First published in the UK 2022 by Sona Books
an imprint of Danann Media Publishing Ltd.

CAT NO: **SON0542**
ISBN: **978-1-915343-03-1**

Made in EU.

Welcome to

The Complete Beginner's Guide to

Embroidery

There's something therapeutic about taking a piece of fabric and turning it into something wonderful. Whether you're adorning it with a flowery motif, cross stitching the name of a newborn or creating something colourful for your wall, the punching of the needle through a fat quarter or Aida and the rustle of the thread that follows is incredibly calming.

In *The Complete Beginner's Guide to Embroidery*, you can experience this for yourself. Regardless of if you're a needlework novice or a seasoned sewer, we've laid out all the tools and techniques you need to get started. The wide range of projects you'll find in these pages mean that you'll never be short of gifts for birthdays, holidays, Christenings or those 'just because' moments. So what are you waiting for? Grab your needle and thread, that all-important cup of tea, and turn the page to learn all about the magical world of embroidery.

CONTENTS

Getting Started

16 Beginner Projects

46

The Next Step

98

Tricky Techniques

Getting Started

Everything you need to begin your journey in embroidery

YOUR BASIC EMBROIDERY TOOL KIT OVER PAGE

Your basic embroidery tool kit

Fill your sewing box with the essentials and you're good to go, then it's just a case of choosing your first project

Before you start your embroidery, it pays to make sure you have everything to hand. As you gain experience and learn new skills, there are lots more tools and items that you can add, but everyone's basic embroidery kit should include:

Crewel embroidery needles have a long eye, making them easy to thread. They come in sizes 1-10: the higher the number, the finer the needle. It's good to stock up so you have a couple of sizes in your stash.

Stranded cotton embroidery threads come in 'skeins' of mercerised cotton. The skeins, which are available in a huge range of colours, are made up of six strands of thread, which can be used singly or in multiples. Three strands are used in most embroideries.

Needle threaders come in handy when you're using very fine thread with small needles.

Embroidery hoops keep the work taut and provide an instant frame to display when it's finished. Work with a hoop that is about 3cm larger than the design you're working on or, for larger projects, recentre the hoop as you go.

Embroidery scissors are smaller than regular shears, with a very fine tip that's perfect for cutting close to your knotted thread ends.

Fabric Most fabrics can be embroidered, but even-weave linen or cotton are traditional embroidery cloths that are easy to work with. If your fabric is thin, slip a layer of white cotton lawn or voile underneath it to add density and treat it as one when stitching. For more advanced projects on thicker fabrics, like denim or felt, use a thimble to take the strain instead.

Erasable pens are a speedy method of mark making that fades over time. Water-soluble types should disappear after a wash, but be sure to double check on a scrap before applying to your fabric. Chalk pens, pencils and carbon paper are good options, too.

Sewing machine with standard feet (regular, zip and buttonhole). Keep a few spare sewing-machine needles at the ready. A free-motion embroidery foot will come in handy for your future projects, too.

Sewing thread Go for good quality, all-purpose polyester or cotton thread in a variety of colours.

Tape measure Choose one with metal ends so it's nice and sturdy.

Pins It's good to have a selection from extra long to extra fine.

Iron and ironing board to press any creases from your fabric once removed from the embroidery hoop.

Using an embroidery hoop

An embroidery hoop will keep the fabric taut, and help prevent puckering. To stop the fabric slipping as you stitch, and prevent the hoop marking the fabric, bind the inner ring with white cotton tape before you begin. Hold tape in place with masking tape, then overlap ends of binding and secure with a few stitches.

Lay the inner ring flat on your surface and place the fabric on top with the pattern positioned within the ring. Loosen the tension screw on the outer ring and press it over the inner ring, capturing the fabric. Tighten the screw to secure rings together, making sure the fabric is smooth and the fabric grain straight.

Photos Future Plc

Transferring an embroidery pattern

4 different ways to get a design onto your fabric

1 Trace the motif outline onto a piece of tracing paper with a fine black felt pen. Turn the tracing over and redraw the motif with a 2B pencil. Place the tracing, pencil side down, onto your fabric. Don't place it too close to the corner or edge of your fabric or you won't be able to fit it in the embroidery hoop. Redraw the design with a sharp HB pencil to transfer the outlines to the fabric.

2 Trace the template onto a water-soluble stabiliser, then place over your fabric. Stitch the design through both the stabiliser and fabric. Once complete, gently soak the embroidery in warm water and the stabiliser will dissolve.

3 Place carbon transfer paper over the fabric and position a photocopy of the template over the top. Using a blunt pencil, trace the design, leaving a carbon copy underneath on the fabric.

4 Create a design that's completely unique to you by copying the motif by eye using an air or water erasable pen.

Stitching tips

- Cut your fabric 7-8cm bigger all round than the finished design area. To help keep an even tension, place your fabric in an embroidery hoop. However, do not leave the piece in there between working on it or it will crease.
- Before you start, locate the centre of the fabric by gently folding in half, then in half again. Mark the spot with a water-soluble pen. Begin stitching your design from this point.
- Working from a chart? Each coloured square on the chart represents one cross stitch. Follow the chart as you stitch, counting the number of stitches for each colour.
- Embroidery thread is usually made up of six strands. Check your chart to see how many strands are required for your design, then separate by cutting a length roughly 45cm (or the length up to your elbow) and gently pulling out the strands you require.
- Use short lengths of thread, no longer than 30cm, to reduce the chance of creating knots and tangles.
- At the start and finish of each thread, run your threaded needle under a few stitches on the back of the fabric to secure and snip off excess thread. This will result in a smooth, knot-free reverse.

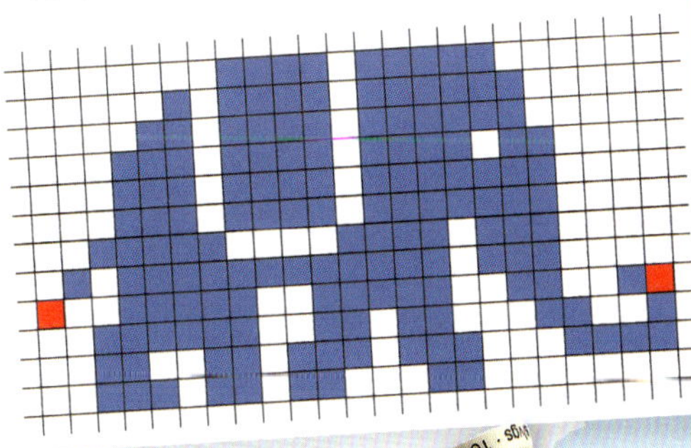

Embroidery stitch guide

All the stitches and techniques you will need to make our projects

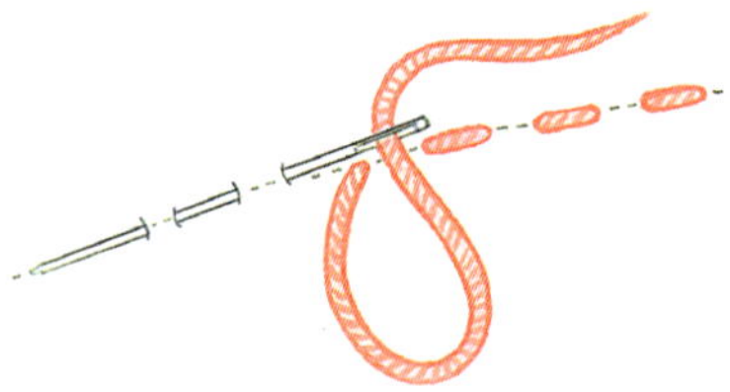

Running stitch

Take the needle in and out of the fabric to form small, straight stitches, evenly spaced and of equal length, along the desired line.

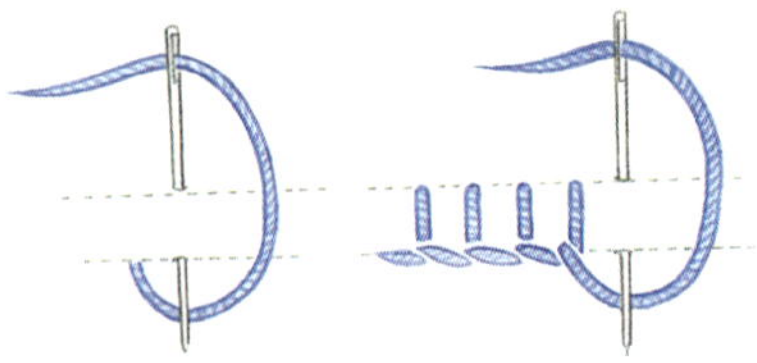

Blanket stitch

Bring the needle out at 1, reinsert at 2, then — trapping the thread under the needle — out at 3. Gently pull the loop taut, then re-insert needle at 4, ready for the next stitch.

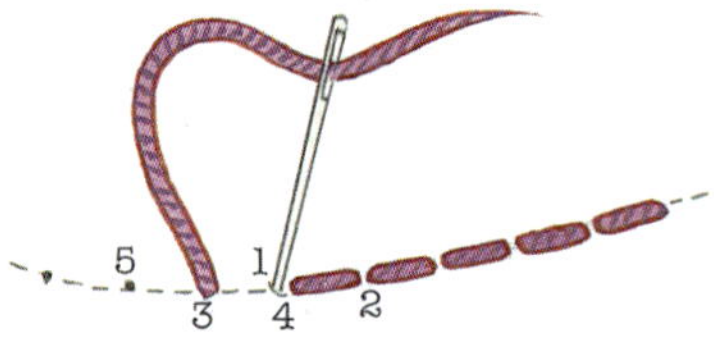

Back stitch

Work from right to left, bringing the needle up at 1, down at 2, up at 3, down at 4, up at 5, and so on.

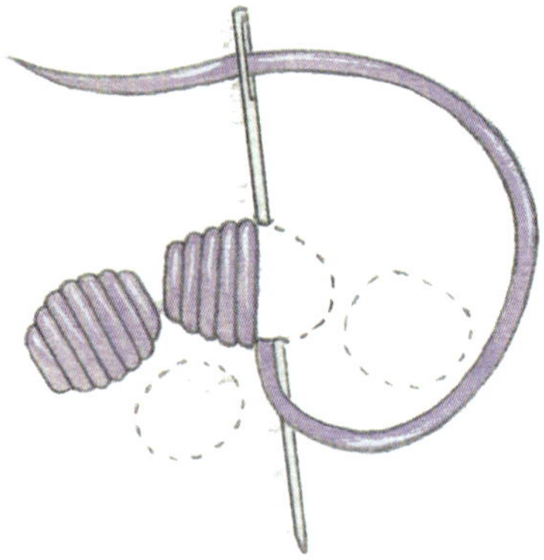

Satin stitch

Work straight, parallel stitches closely together to cover an area — there should be no gaps between stitches.

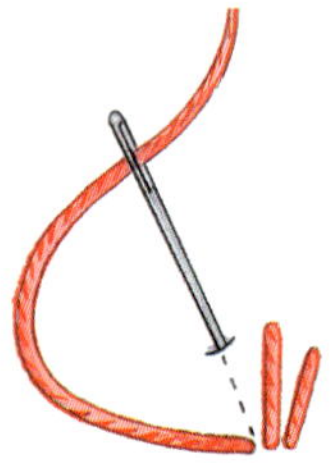

Straight stitch

Simply bring the needle through and reinsert at the positions indicated on the chart, making one long stitch. Straight stitches can be any length, from quite short to very long.

Threaded running stitch

Work a line of running stitch, then thread a second thread through. This second thread doesn't go through the fabric, it just weaves through the stitches.

Looped back stitch

Backstitch can be simply threaded as in threaded running stitch. For more effect, loop a contrasting thread through the stitches as in the diagram.

Scallop stitch

Sew a loose stitch from 1 to 2, and bring the needle up at 3. Reinsert needle at 4, trapping the loose thread into a scallop. Bring the needle out next to 2, ready for the next stitch.

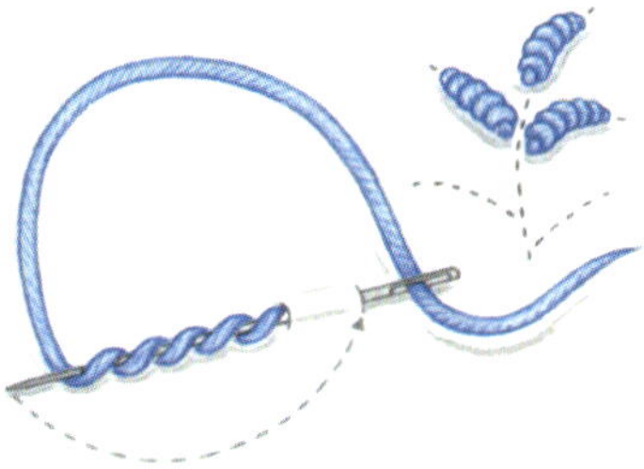

Bullion knot

Bring needle through from back to face side of fabric at end of where you want the bullion knot to start. Make a backstitch, the size of the bullion stitch required, and bring the needle point out where it first emerged through the fabric. Wind thread round the needle point, as many times as required to equal the space of the backstitch. Hold left thumb on coiled thread and pull needle through; still holding the coiled thread, turn needle back to where it was inserted and insert in same place. Pull thread through until bullion stitch lies fat. Use a needle with a small eye to allow thread to pass through the coil easily.

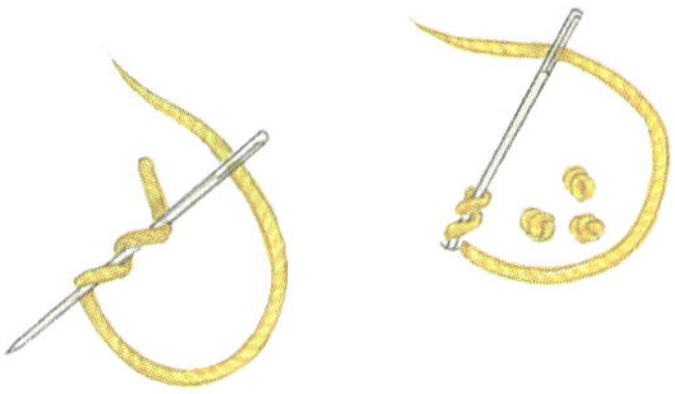

French knot

Bring the thread up through the fabric, hold it with the thumb and first finger of your left hand and turn the needle round it once or twice or as necessary. Still holding the thread firmly with your left hand, turn the needle and reinsert it close to the point where it first emerged. Pull the thread taut so the knot slides down the needle to touch the fabric, then release as the needle goes through the fabric leaving the knot on the surface.

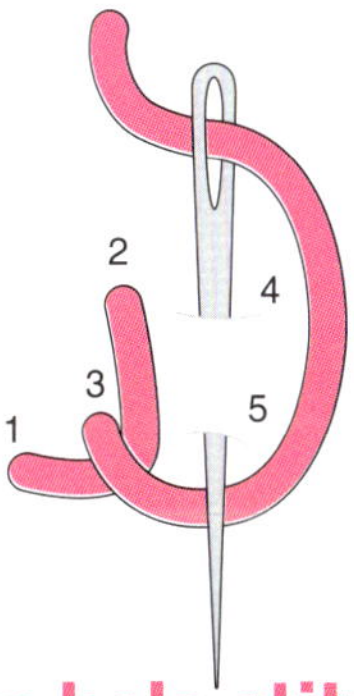

Button hole stitch

Working from left to right, bring the needle out to the front of the fabric very close to the outline edge. Put the needle back a small distance above the edge and slightly to the right, bringing it out again at the edge below with the tip of the needle over the working thread. Pull the thread through and repeat to form an almost solid line of stitches.

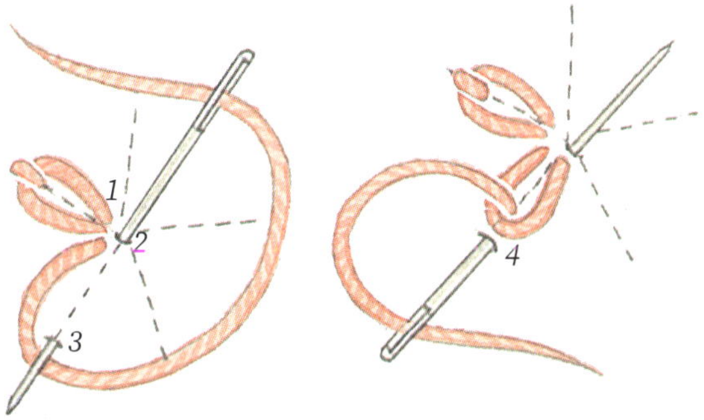

Lazy daisy

Make a circle of detached chain stitches to form a fower. Bring the needle out at 1, reinsert beside 1 at 2, bring half out at 3 looping thread round needle point to form a petal. Complete a small stitch at 4, securing petal shape, then bring out ready for the next stitch.

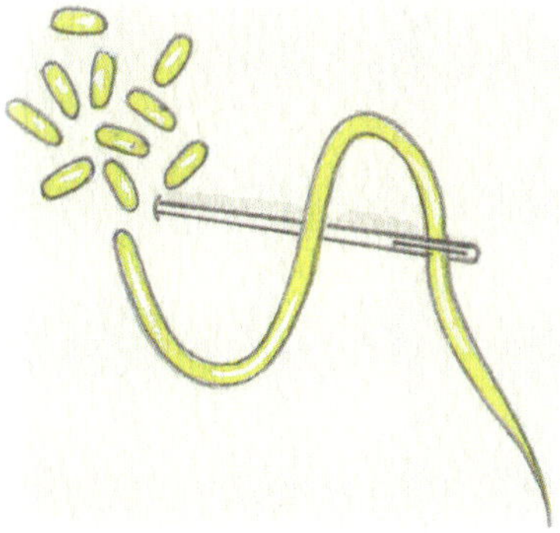

Seed stitch

Work small, short straight stitches at different angles to fill the area required.

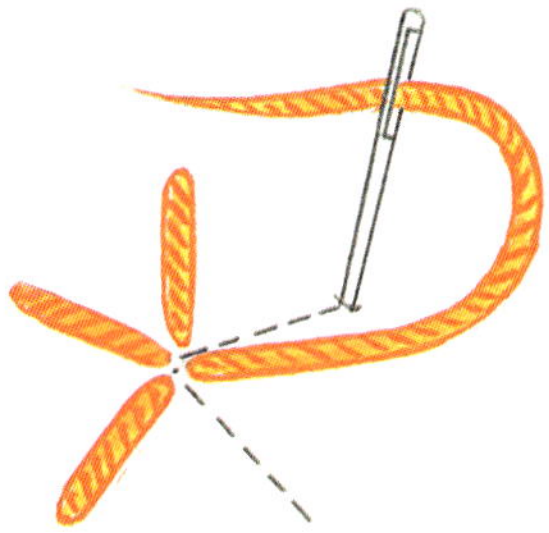

Straight stitch star

Straight stitches, of the same or varying lengths, can be used to form stars, tassels, or other shapes.

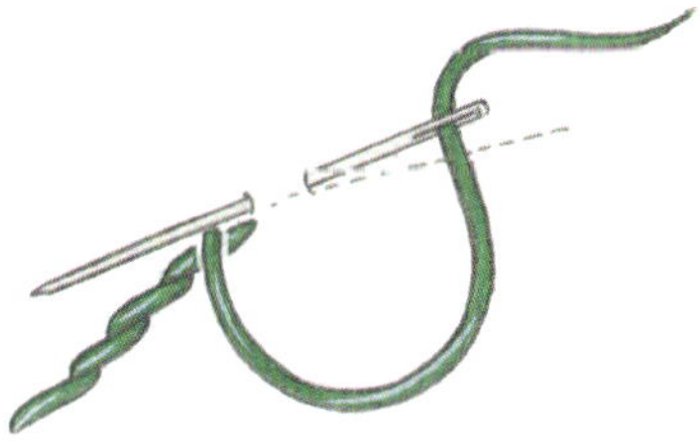

Stem stitch

Work from left to right (reverse if you are left-handed). Bring the needle up at the end of the line and make a short stitch, bringing the needle up again immediately adjacent to the first stitch and about halfway down its length, make another stitch the same length as the first and repeat to make a line of stepped stitches in this way.

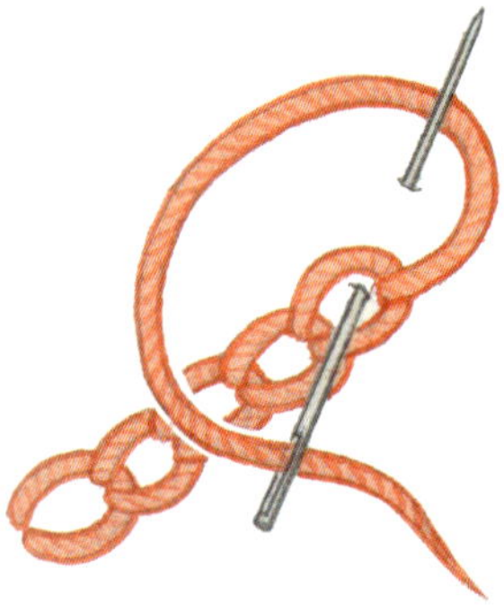

Chain stitch

Bring the needle out at the end of the stitching line. Reinsert at the same point and bring out a short distance away, looping the thread around the needle tip. Pull the thread through. To begin the next stitch, insert the needle at the point where it last emerged, just inside the loop of the previous stitch, and bring out a short distance away, again looping thread around the needle. Continue in the same way.

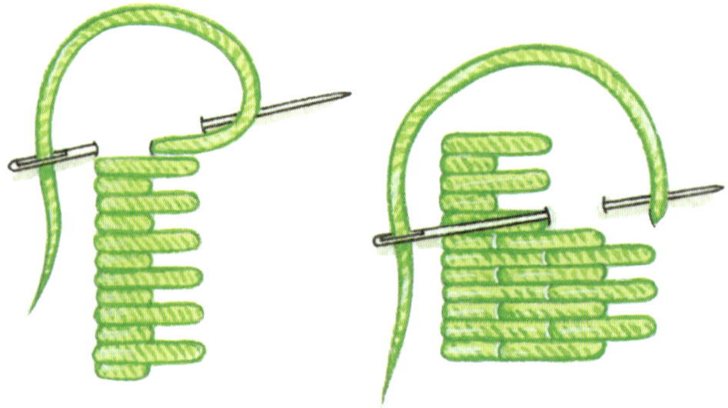

Long and short stitch

Starting at the outside edge, stitch long and short stitches alternately. Stitch subsequent rows of equal length stitches. You may need to leave out some stitches to fill the shape neatly.

Counted thread stitches

Cross stitch

To work cross stitch, bring the needle through at the lower left-hand side, insert the needle one block up and one block to the right and bring it out one block down, forming a diagonal stitch. Continue in this way to form a row of stitches.

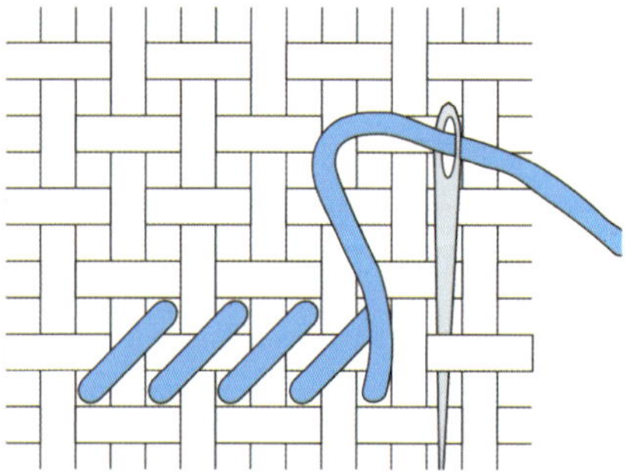

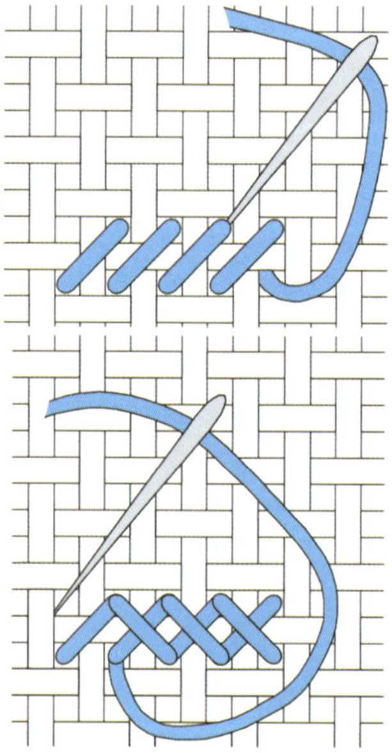

Complete the upper half of the crosses as shown. Cross stitch may be worked from right to left or vice versa, but the upper half of all the crosses must lie in the same direction.

Back stitch

Bring the needle through at the corner of a stitch (1), then take a backward stitch over one block (2). Bring the needle through one block in front of the first stitch (3). Then take another stitch, reinserting the needle where it first came through the fabric (1). Continue to make a row.

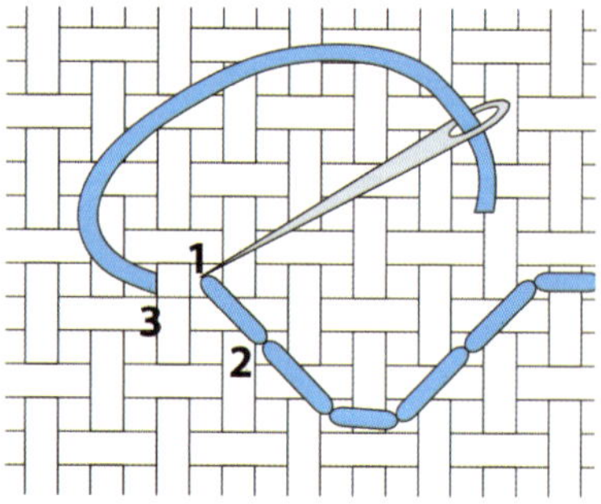

Always work the backstitches one block in length, noting that the stitching doesn't have to be in a straight line — it can be worked in different directions, down the side of blocks or even diagonally across a block.

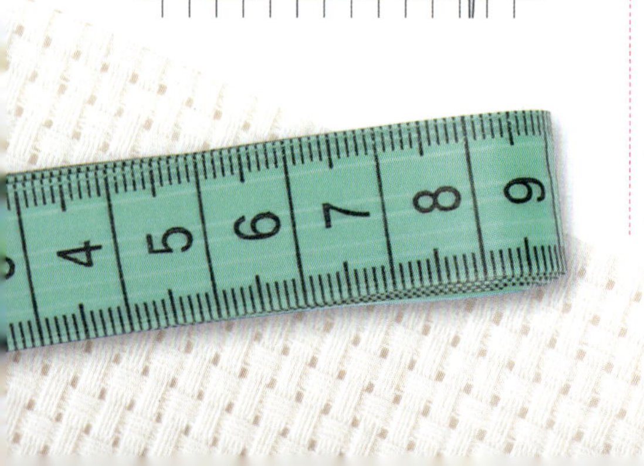

Basic hand stitches

Over stitch

Overcast or oversewing is the customary hand stitch for finishing raw edges of fabric to prevent them from fraying. Working from either direction, take diagonal stitches over the edge, spacing them an even distance apart at a uniform depth.

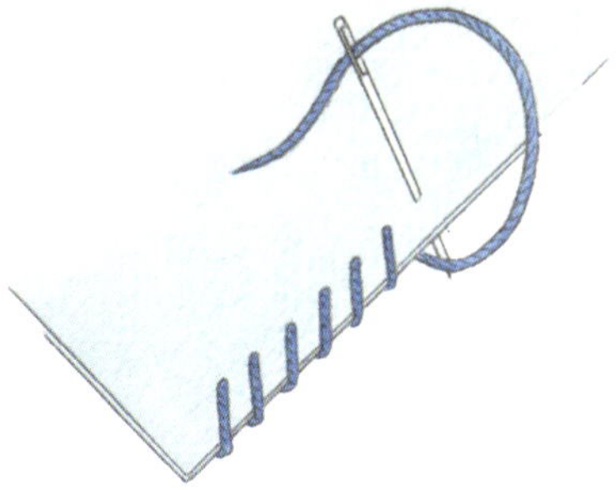

Whip stitch

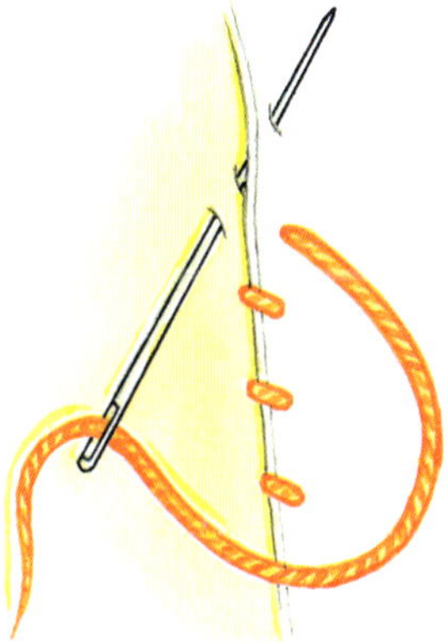

This stitch is used to hold two finished edges together. Working from right to left, bring the needle out through the top layer of fabric close to the edge. Take the needle diagonally to the left and insert it in the lower layer of fabric and bring it back out through the top layer diagonally to the left, creating a slanting stitch. Continue in this way until the two edges are joined. The slanted stitches that are produced can be short or long, depending on how close you stitch to the edge of the top layer of fabric.

Slip stitch

This stitch is used to join two folded edges together. Working from right to left, bring the needle out through one folded edge. For the first stitch and each following stitch, slip the needle through the fold of the opposite edge for about 6mm; bring the needle out and draw the thread through. Continue to slip the needle and thread through the opposing folded edges until the seam is closed.

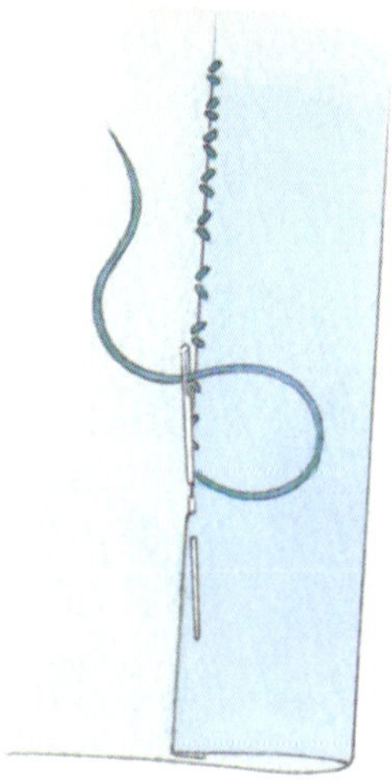

Free machine embroidery

- Use this style of embroidery to 'draw' details on to a project with the sewing-machine needle and to 'colour in' areas. You can go over stitching several times to give a sketchy, scribbled look; it doesn't have to be neat to give a great effect.
- If you haven't tried free-machine embroidery before, practise first on scraps of fabric. To embroider, you will need to adjust your sewing machine by dropping the feed dogs (these are the teeth that come up through the needle plate as you sew and move the fabric along in a straight line); refer to your sewing-machine manual to do this.
- You will also need a free-machine embroidery foot, sometimes called a darning or a free-motion foot. This stops the fabric from lifting while you sew. You might also find it helpful to fit the fabric into an embroidery hoop while you sew to keep the fabric flat and taut and prevent any puckering.
- Once you're ready, set the stitch length on the machine to zero. You will need to move the fabric around manually to create the stitches, otherwise you will just sew on the spot, so start slowly to get the feel of the stitching, and see how fast you need to move the fabric to achieve the look you want. Think of the fabric as a piece of paper and the needle as a pencil and reverse it in your mind so you're moving the paper (fabric) to make the design.

TOP TIP

Be very careful to keep your fingers away from the needle as you move the fabric about under it, as it can be easy to catch your finger under the needle.

28
m
42
HL
34
40
Bee happy
STRETCH FABRICS ONLY

Beginner Projects

The perfect projects for anyone just starting out with needlework

Little drops of happiness

Create cushions and a matching purse that will brighten any cloudy day

You will need

Cloud and raindrop cushions

- Access to a photocopier
- Spot and striped fabrics
- Black tapestry wool and needle
- Pins
- Sewing machine
- Polyester stuffing
- Needle and cotton thread

Cloud purse

- Access to a photocopier
- 25cm square of turquoise felt
- 25cm square of turquoise cotton fabric
- White stranded cotton embroidery thread
- White 10cm zip
- Matching sewing thread

Makes: Suzie Attaway, Cheryl Owen and Emily Dawe

Cloud and raindrop cushions

Finished size: Cloud cushion 50 x 28cm; raindrop cushions 26 x 16cm and 22 x 14.5cm

Making the cushions

1 Enlarge the cloud template on a photocopier by 400%. Place on top of two different pieces of spot and stripe fabric. Next, draw around the template with a pencil, and cut out two pieces. Set one cloud piece aside.

2 Lightly draw two eyes and a mouth on to the middle of one cloud piece with a pencil. Stitch over with black tapestry wool.

3 Place the two cloud pieces, right sides together, pin and sew around the edges taking a 1cm seam allowance, leaving a

Cloud template

Enlarge by 400% on a photocopier for cloud cushion
Enlarge by 160% on a photocopier for cloud purse

Raindrop template

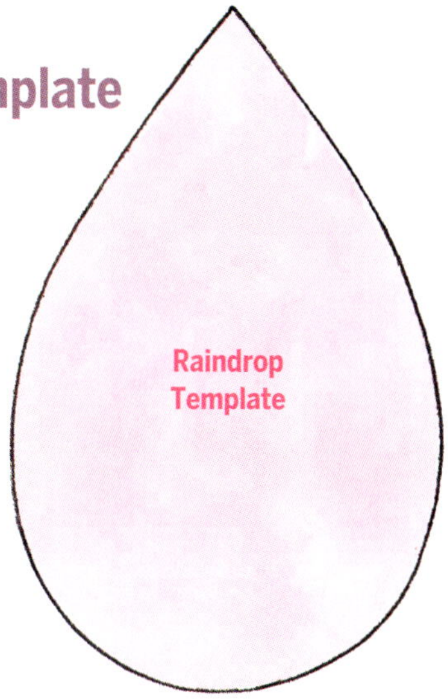

Enlarge by 400% and 370% on a photocopier

small opening along the bottom. Turn the cloud right side out, and fill with polyester stuffing. Stitch the opening closed.

4 Repeat with the raindrop template, enlarging by 200%, then 200% and 200% then 170% respectively, to make the raindrop cushions.

Cloud purse

Finished size: 14 x 8cm

Making paper patterns

Enlarge the cloud template on a photocopier by 160% and cut out. Use the pattern to cut out one pair of clouds from felt and one pair of linings from turquoise cotton. Cut two 5 x 2.5cm rectangles from felt for the zip end covers.

Embroidering the cloud

Draw the raindrops on the wrong side of the pattern with a pencil. Place the pattern right side up on one felt cloud. Redraw the raindrops to transfer them to the felt. Embroider the raindrops onto the purse with four strands of white embroidery thread using satin stitch.

Making the purse

1 Press under 1cm on the short edges of the zip end covers. Press the covers in half parallel with the pressed edges with wrong sides facing. Trim an equal amount off each end of the zip to make the length of 12.5cm.

2 Slip each end of the zip into a zip end cover with the raw edges of the covers level with the long edges of the zip. Tack in place through all of the layers.

3 With the zip centred and right sides facing, pin one long edge of the zip to one long edge of the embroidered cloud with right sides facing. Use a zipper foot to stitch in place, taking a 1.5cm seam allowance. Repeat to stitch the other long edge of the zip to the other felt cloud. Press the clouds away from the zip. Topstitch close to the zip teeth.

4 Open the zip. Pin the felt clouds together with right sides facing. Stitch the raw edges, taking a 5mm seam allowance. Clip corners and snip the curves. Finger press the seam open.

5 Press under 1cm on the straight edges of the linings. With right sides facing, pin and stitch the linings together along the raw edges, taking a 5mm seam allowance. Snip the curves and finger press the seam open. Turn the lining right side out. Insert the purse into the lining, matching the ends of the seams.

6 Pin and slip stitch the pressed edges of the lining to the zip and upper corners of the purse. Turn the purse right side out.

Feature and styling: Linda McClelland. Photography: Sussie Bell. Makes: Cheryl Owen

Owl cross stitch card

Send this gorgeous handmade card to say thank you, happy birthday, welcome new baby or simply hello

To work the embroidery

1 Mount the Aida fabric securely in the embroidery hoop; this will keep the work taut, making it easier to handle while stitching and helping to minimise any distortion.

2 The design is worked only in cross stitch. If you're a beginner, practise a few stitches first on some spare fabric.

3 The design chart shows the complete design for our owl card. Each coloured square on the chart represents one cross stitch, and the cross-stitch key indicates the colour of wool to be used.

4 Using two strands of stranded embroidery thread and an embroidery needle, refer to the chart, key and stitch guide to stitch the design.

To make the card

1 Once completed, cut out the cross-stitch design leaving a four-square-deep border on all edges beyond the outline shown on the chart. Carefully pull away the threads of the fabric to fray the border.

2 Score across the centre of the card parallel with the short edges. Fold the card in half along the scored line. Stick the design centrally to the front of the card with double-sided sticky tape 3.5cm below the upper edge.

TOP TIP

Ask for embroidery thread by code number rather than colour. The colours are given only a guide.

You will need

Owl cross stitch card

- 20cm square piece of white 14-count Aida
- Anchor stranded embroidery thread in the following colours:
- 1 skein each of:
- 1090 (Turquoise)
- 170 (Deep blue)
- 253 (Light green)
- 225 (Mid green)
- 189 (Jade green)
- Masking tape
- Embroidery needle
- Embroidery hoop
- 24 x 15cm rectangle of light blue card
- Double-sided sticky tape
- Scissors
- Craft knife and ruler

Design chart & stitch guide

Key:

- 1090 (Turquoise)
- 253 (Light green)
- 189 (Jade green)
- 170 (Deep blue)
- 225 (Mid geen)

Winter warmer

Make your own hot water bottle this winter

You will need

For a 22 x 34cm hot water bottle

- 30 x 85cm piece wool felt in mustard
- A4 sheet of wool felt in white
- Embroidery thread in white
- Embroidery needle
- Scissors
- Pins
- 2ltr hot water bottle
- Paper and pencil
- Ruler

1 Place your empty hot water bottle on a piece of paper and use a pencil to draw around the edge. With a ruler, straighten the lines at the neck of the bottle, using our image as a guide. Add 2cm around all the edges of the hot water bottle to create your front hot water bottle template.

2 For the two back templates, measure 28cm up from the bottom of the template. Draw a horizontal dashed line to mark this length. Then measure 18cm down from the top of the template and draw a horizontal dotted line to mark this length.

3 Cut out the template and pin to the mustard wool felt. Cut out one front and one of each of the back pieces.

4 For the two back pieces, turn the edges with the dashed lines under by 1cm and then another 1cm to create a double hem. Pin and topstitch in place with matching sewing thread. Blanket stitch over the sewn edges with six strands of white embroidery thread and an embroidery needle.

5 To create the personalised letter on the front, either draw your letter onto a piece of paper with a pencil or print it out on a computer. Cut out the letter motif, pin to the white wool felt and then cut out around the paper.

Cover back

6 Pin the letter in the centre of the front hot water bottle piece and blanket stitch around the edge to secure. Alternatively, if you're short on time, you can always use a zigzag stitch on your sewing machine to sew the appliqué in place.

7 Pin the front hot water bottle piece to the back pieces with right sides together and pin all the way around the edge, making sure the two back pieces overlap to form the opening. Sew the pieces together with a 1cm seam allowance. Clip into the curves, turn right sides out and press.

Words and make: Esme Clemo. Photos: Barry Marsden

Gemstone mobile

Diamonds are a girl's best friend when it comes to our jewel-coloured felt hanging

You will need

Jewel mobile

- Transfer paper
- Coloured felt
- Embroidery thread (hoop optional)
- Toy stuffing
- Small faceted beads
- Your basic sewing kit

a

b

1 Using the templates on page 25 and transfer paper, mark the shapes onto felt with a pencil (a). Place motifs in hoop, if preferred, then using three strands of contrasting embroidery thread, work around the design in back stitch (b). Repeat for all seven shapes.

2 Leaving a 1cm border round each shape, cut around the designs. Cut out a matching back for each shape (c). Pair wrong sides facing and work around the edges in running stitch, using two strands of coordinating embroidery thread, leaving a small gap. Fill with a little stuffing (d), then sew up the gap. Repeat for all the shapes.

3 Cut a length of white sewing thread and stitch to the top of the teardrop shape. Add three small coloured beads, then measure 3cm up and sew to the bottom of the bullet shape (e). Cut more thread and sew to the top of the bullet. Add three more beads, then stitch to the bottom point of the large diamond, 3cm down.

4 Repeat to attach the octagon to the emerald shape with 3cm of thread, then attach these to the left-hand side of the big diamond with 6cm of thread. In the same way, sew the star to the oval, then the oval to the right-hand side of the diamond (f). Finally, sew a loop of thread to the top of the diamond for hanging, adding several more beads if desired.

c

d

e

f

Gemstone mobile templates

Use transfer paper to mark the shapes onto felt

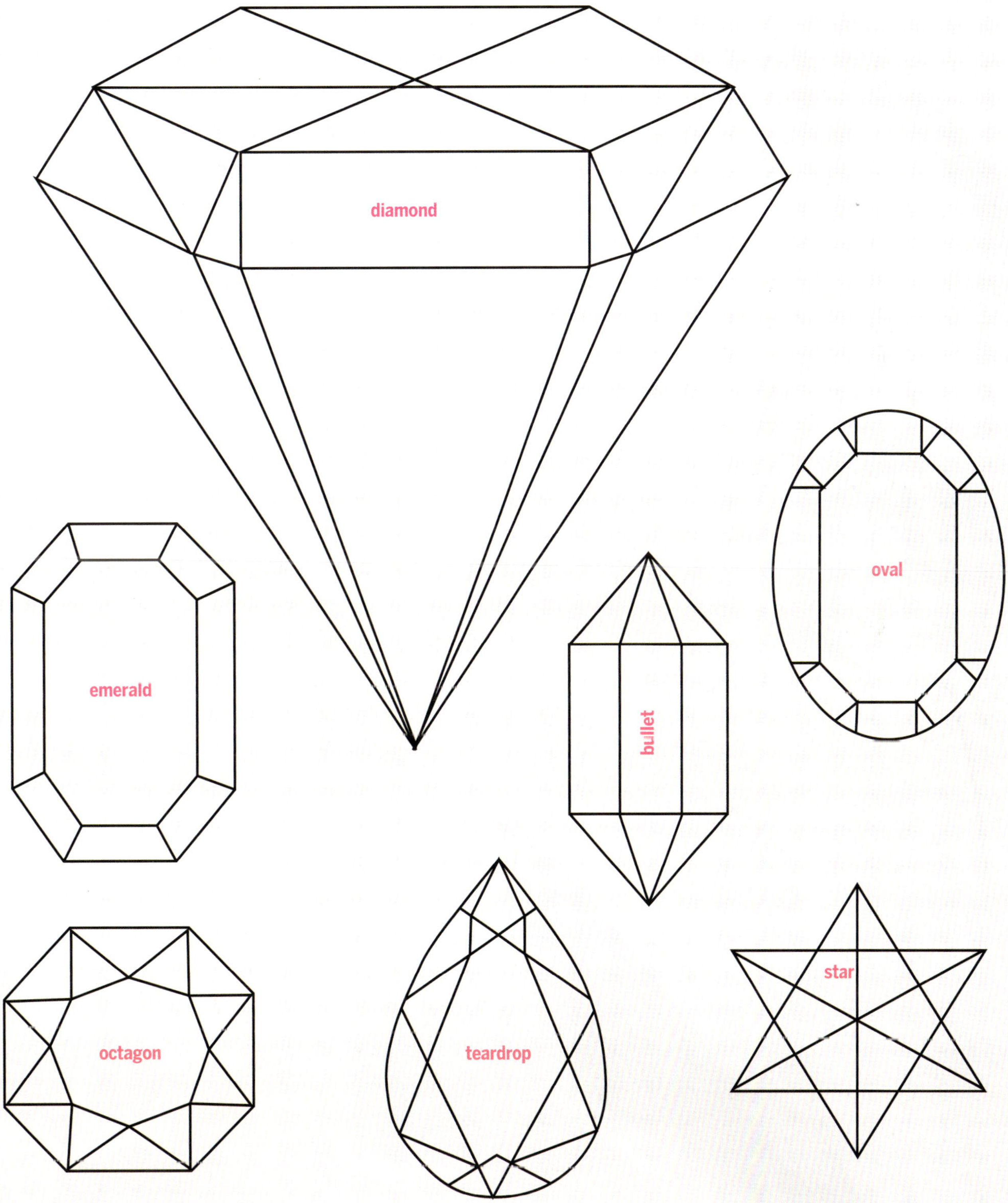

Project & step photos Stephanie Durrant Photo Claire Lloyd Davies

Makes and words: Esme Clemo. Photo: Barry Marsden

You will need

For two cushions

- 50cm x 1m patterned cotton fabric in green and pink
- 30 x 30cm sheet of felt in pink and green
- 2m flanged piping cord in green and pink
- Matching sewing thread
- Matching embroidery thread
- Embroidery needle
- Two 43cm square cushion pads

Love letters

Personalise a cushion or two with this blanket-stitch appliqué

1 Cut a 45cm square and two 31.5 x 45cm rectangles from the patterned pink or green fabric.

2 Using a computer, print and cut out a letter of your choice in a solid font to create your template — we used Georgia typeface. Trace around the letter template onto the green or pink felt and cut out.

3 Pin the appliqué letter to the front of the patterned fabric square using our photo as your colour guide. With three strands of contrasting embroidery thread, blanket stitch around the edge of the letter.

4 Lay the piping on to the right side of the front cushion cover piece with raw edges matching. Pin in place, starting and finishing on the same edge of the cushion, and snipping into seam allowances of the piping to help it turn the corners.

5 Stitch the piping in place, using a zipper foot and leaving a gap at the ends of the piping cord. To join the ends of the piping, unpick a few stitches on the piping fabric strip and trim the two cord ends so that they butt. Turn under 1cm of fabric at one end of the piping to neaten it and slip this end over the raw end. Hand stitch ends neatly in place, then machine this section in place.

6 Turn one of the long edges on each of the patterned fabric rectangles under by 1cm and then another 1cm. Pin and stitch to secure.

7 Pin the two patterned rectangles to the patterned square with right sides facing so that the rectangles overlap. Sew all the way around the edge with a 1.5cm seam allowance. Turn right sides out, press and stuff with a cushion pad.

Needle case

Our Skandi-inspired felt case will keep all your pins and needles neat and tidy — and you can even stitch an initial to personalise it

Your stitch guide

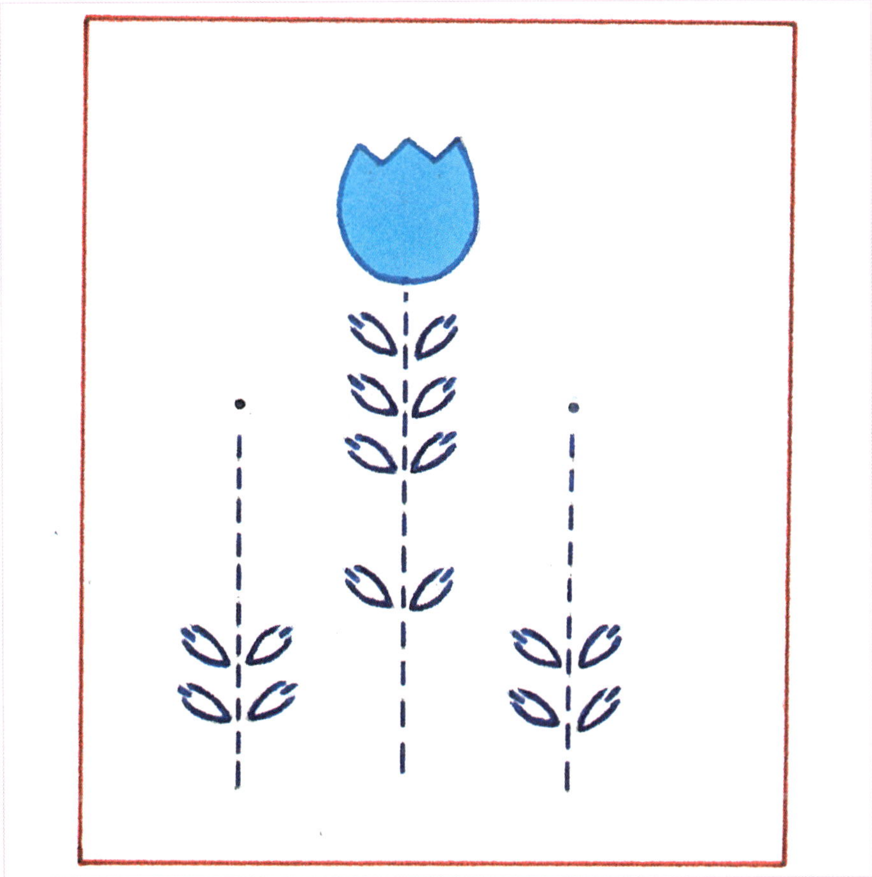

Actual-size pattern

Make: Cheryl Owen. Styling: Emily Dawe. Photos: Sussie Bell

You will need

Finished size: 10.5 x 9cm

- Tracing paper and sharp HB pencil
- 25 x 20cm rectangle of red felt
- 15cm square of turquoise patterned cotton fabric
- 3cm square of turquoise felt
- 3cm square of bonding web
- 20cm square of white felt
- Two 1cm white buttons
- Navy stranded cotton embroidery thread
- Matching sewing threads

Cutting out

1 Cut the red felt into four equal pieces. Cut four 9.5 x 8.5cm rectangles for the pages from white felt. Cut one 12 x 5.5cm bias strip for the binding from patterned fabric.

2 Trace the tulip onto the paper backing of the bonding web. Press the bonding web onto turquoise felt. Cut out the tulip neatly. Peel off the backing paper. Refer to the pattern to press the tulip onto one cover, this will be the front.

Making the needle case

1 Refer to the pattern to draw the stems on the front with a sharp pencil. Using three strands of navy embroidery thread, embroider the stems with stem stitch and the leaves with lazy daisy stitches. Sew a button at the dots with navy embroidery thread.

2 With the embroidery facing up, pin the front and another cover together. Pin the other two covers together for the back. Topstitch close to the short edges and the long right-hand edge.

3 Pile the pages together on the back, matching the long left-hand edges with the back extending evenly at the top, bottom and right-hand edge. Place the front on top. Tack the left-hand edges together.

4 Press the binding lengthwise in half with wrong sides facing. Pin the binding to the left-hand edge of the front, with the ends extending beyond the top and bottom edges. Stitch through the layers taking a 0.75mm seam allowance.

5 Pin the ends of the binding over the top and bottom of the case. Fold the pressed edge over the layers and pin along the seam. Slipstitch in place.

STAR BAKER

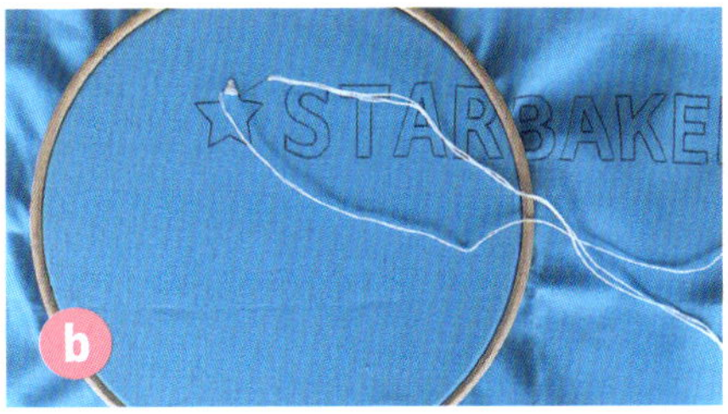

Project & step photos Esme Clemo Photos Simon Whitmore

Star baker

Whip up some stitching for the kitchen with this Great British Bake Off-inspired make

You will need

Cake wrap

- 20 x 50cm Brush Strokes fabric
- 20 x 35cm teal cotton
- 8 x 32cm Vlieseline lightweight fusible interfacing
- White embroidery thread skein
- 1m yellow ric rac
- Embroidery hoop and needle
- Star Baker template
- Your basic sewing kit
- Vanishing marker

1 Cut the teal fabric in half to make two 10 x 34cm rectangles (or you might want to cut your fabric after it's been embroidered so you can work the fabric in an embroidery hoop). Trace the Star Baker template (below) onto one of the teal rectangles with a vanishing marker (a).

2 Place the fabric in a hoop, if preferred, and stitch the stars and letters in satin stitch (b). Following the outlines of the shapes, work straight stitches close together. Keep tension even and stitches close for a smooth finish with no background fabric visible. Tie a knot on reverse of the piece to secure (c). Remove the embroidered fabric from hoop and press on reverse.

3 Cut the ric rac into four strips, two measuring 10cm and two measuring 34cm. On the right sides, pin and topstitch to the corresponding sides (d). Fuse interfacing to the reverse of the embroidered fabric, making sure to follow the manufacturer's instructions.

4 Cut the patterned fabric into two 10 x 50cm strips. Turn one of the short and two long sides under by 1cm and topstitch.

5 Pin the patterned strips to the short sides of the teal rectangle and layer the embroidered section on top with right sides together (e). Sew with a 1cm seam allowance, leaving one of the short ends unstitched for turning. Turn out, press and slipstitch the gap closed.

Star baker template

★ STAR BAKER ★

Enlarge by 140% on a photocopier

Leaf wash bag

Store your make-up or toiletries in this handy homemade wash bag

Makes and words: Esme Clemo. Photo: Barry Marsden

You will need

Wash bag

- 20cm metal zip
- 20cm square of green fabric
- 50 x 50cm pale pink stripe fabric
- Matching sewing thread
- Hand-sewing needle
- Paper-backed adhesive webbing
- Pins and scissors
- Pink embroidery threads
- Small tassel maker
- Embroidery needle

Leaf template

Actual-size pattern

1 Photocopy the monstera leaf template and cut out. Fuse the webbing to the green fabric and trace around the template onto the paper backing. Cut out and repeat until you have four leaves.

2 Cut the pink stripe fabric into four 20 x 25cm rectangles — two for the front and two for the lining — and two 4cm squares for the zip tabs. Place two leaf appliqués onto the front washbag pieces, remove the paper backing, and fuse in place.

3 With your sewing machine set to a small straight stitch, sew around the edge of each monstera leaf in a contrasting sewing thread.

4 Fold the zip tabs in half, then unfold and press the sides to the fold line. Trim the zip ends so they measure 1cm from the zip stopper and pull. Sandwich the zip ends inside the fabric zip tabs and, using a zipper foot on your sewing machine, stitch in place as close to the fold as possible.

5 With one of the appliqué pieces right side up, pin the zip wrong side down on top followed by a lining piece so the edge of the fabrics align with the edge of the zip tape. Using the zipper foot, sew the pinned edge with a 1cm seam allowance. Repeat for the other side of the zip with the other pieces of fabric.

6 Press the zip seams flat with right sides facing up and then topstitch about 5mm from the zip teeth using the zipper foot.

7 Open the zip. Pin the lining pieces together with right sides facing and the front pieces together with right sides facing. Stitch the sides first, always starting with the lining and sewing towards the front pieces, with a 1.5cm seam allowance.

8 Sew the bottom of the front pieces with a 1.5cm seam allowance and repeat for the lining, leaving a 10cm gap in the centre for turning through.

9 Trim the corners and turn the bag right sides out. Turn the raw edges of the opening on the lining in by 1.5cm seam allowance and slip stitch closed, or sew with a machine for speed.

10 Wind the pink embroidery threads around the tassel maker to create two small tassels. Thread an embroidery needle with a 10cm length of embroidery thread, guide through the tops of the tassels and tie to the zip pull. Guide the needle through the centre of the tassels to disguise the tail ends and then trim the bottoms of the tassels.

Baby love

This monogrammed cushion is the perfect gift for a newborn's christening and will look pretty on display in a nursery

You will need

Monogrammed cushion

- Tracing paper and pencil
- Iron-on transfer pen
- 15 x 15cm white cotton or linen fabric for the front
- Two quilters fat quarters in a colourful print
- Stranded embroidery cotton to complement print fabric
- Embroidery hoop
- Crewel needle
- 1m flanged piping cord in white or cream
- Matching sewing thread
- Zipper or piping foot
- Polyester toy stuffing

Makes: Suzie Attaway, Cheryl Owen and Emily Dawe

Cutting out

For one pillow, cut two strips of 7 x 15cm and two of 7 x 25cm fabric in a complementary print. Cut one 25 x 25cm cushion back.

1 Using a computer, print your chosen initials on to a sheet of tracing paper, or draw out the letters freehand. On the reverse of the paper, go over the outlines of the letters with a transfer pen.

2 Position the letters in the centre of the white square panel and press with a hot iron to transfer the design. Stretch the fabric in an embroidery hoop and stitch the letters using a close satin stitch worked by hand in a matching thread. Remove from the hoop and press.

3 With right sides facing and 1cm seam allowances, pin and sew the shortest strips to the sides of the embroidered square. Repeat for the longer strips, and sew them to the top and bottom.

4 Lay the piping on to the right side of the front cushion cover piece with raw edges matching. Pin in place, starting and finishing on the same edge of the cushion, and snipping into seam allowances of the piping to help it turn the corners.

5 Stitch the piping in place, using a zipper foot and leaving a gap at the ends of the piping cord. To join the ends of the piping, unpick a few stitches on the piping fabric strip and trim the two cord ends so that they butt. Turn under 1cm of fabric at one end of the piping to neaten it and slip this end over the raw end. Hand stitch ends neatly in place, then machine this section in place.

6 With right sides together and 1cm seam allowances, pin and sew the cushion front and back together. Use the zipper foot on your sewing machine and work closely to the piping. Leave a short gap on one side for turning through. Turn right sides out, stuff with filling and hand sew the opening edges closed.

Stitch & sow

Garden in style with this beautiful apron that's perfect for storing your seeds and tools while looking smart

You will need

Gardening apron

- Tracing paper
- Transfer pencil
- Embroidery hoop
- Embroidery thread in light green, brown, grey, orange and burgundy
- Embroidery needle
- Embroidery scissors
- 150cm of 10mm-wide green ribbon
- 1m of 25mm-wide green ribbon
- 4m x 150cm heavy cotton fabric in cream
- Matching sewing thread
- Hand-sewing needle
- Scissors

Cutting out

For the waistband

Cut a rectangle measuring 10cm x 150cm from the cream fabric.

For the apron

Cut two rectangles measuring 30cm x 50cm.

For the pockets

Cut three rectangles measuring 10cm x 16cm, 12cm x 16cm, 14cm x 16cm each.

1 Using the transfer pencil and a piece of tracing paper, trace the embroidery designs from the templates on the left. Place the tracing paper on the fabric pockets, tracing side down. With an iron set on low, press the paper to the fabric to transfer the design. Gently peel away the paper to reveal the embroidery design beneath.

2 Place the pocket fabric in an embroidery hoop and tighten until the fabric is taut. Using three strands of embroidery thread, back stitch over all the lines left by the transfer pencil. Bring the needle to the right side of the fabric on the transfer line and make a backward stitch 2mm long. Bring the needle forward under the fabric to emerge 2mm ahead of the first stitch. Make another backward stitch and repeat to create a line of back stitches.

3 Once the gardening designs have been embroidered, remove the fabric from the hoop and press to remove any creases.

4 Turn under the top edge of the pockets by 1cm and press. Pin a piece of 6mm-wide ribbon along the top, 5mm below the turned edge. Topstitch in place with contrasting thread to secure. Turn the side edges under by 1cm, pin and press. Repeat for each pocket.

5 Arrange the pockets on the right side of one of the apron pieces, following our image as a guide. Turn the pockets down so they are right sides facing to the apron, stitch along the bottom edge of the pocket

Feature: Esme Clemo. Photos: Barry Marsden

1cm from the pocket edge, and then flip the pocket upwards. The pockets should sit approximately 2cm apart and 6.5cm from the bottom edge. Pin and topstitch the sides to secure the pocket in place.

6 Cut two 6cm lengths of 6mm-wide ribbon and turn under the short ends by 1.5cm. Pin to the apron and stitch across the short ends to secure.

7 Place the apron front and back together with right sides facing and pin around the edges. Sew together with 1cm seam allowances along the side and bottom edges.

8 Take the waistband and topstitch the 25mm wide green ribbon 17mm from the bottom edge. Fold the waistband in half lengthways with right sides together. Pin and stitch along the short ends and side with 1cm seam allowances. Leave a gap in the centre just a little wider than the width of the apron. Turn the waistband right sides out, turn under the edges of the centre gap by 1cm and press. Slip the apron inside the waistband and pin in place. Topstitch the gap closed, stitching close to the turned edge.

Embroidery templates

Use these as a guide for the drawings on the pockets.

Home sweet home

Turn any house into a home with this traditional alphabet cross stitch

You will need

Alphabet cross stitch

- Cross stitch chart on page 39
- Anchor stranded cotton in the following shades: 1021 (Dusty pink), 108 (Lilac) and 186 (Pale jade)
- Tapestry needle size 22
- 30 x 40cm ivory 16-count Aida fabric
- Embroidery hoop

1 Starting from the arrows on the chart, work a row of tacking stitches lengthways and widthways following the bold lines on the chart, across your Aida fabric (the point where the two lines intersect is the centre of the design).

2 Mount your fabric in your embroidery hoop, with the tacked-cross centred. Start stitching from the centre, following the colour key and chart, using three strands of cotton in your needle. Each square on the chart represents one cross-stitch, worked over one block of the fabric (see page 14 for details on how to work this stitch).

3 When the embroidery is finished, remove tacking threads. Place work face down on a padded surface and press on the wrong side, under a damp cloth, using light pressure to avoid flattening the stitches; frame as desired.

Cross stitch chart

Key:

1021 (Dusty pink) 108 (Lilac) 186 (Pale jade)

Words and make: Esme Clemo. Photos: Barry Marsden

Feature Suzie Attaway Styling Jen Morgan

The bee's knees embroidery

Create a handmade picture to brighten up a bare wall

You will need

Bee embroidery

- Embroidery hoop
- Black acrylic paint
- Paintbrush
- Tape measure
- Scissors
- Natural fabric or a napkin
- Pencil
- Tapestry needle
- Yellow, white and black tapestry wool

1 Remove the inner ring from the embroidery hoop and set aside. Paint the outer ring with black acrylic paint and leave to dry completely.

2 Measure and cut a piece of natural fabric slightly larger than the embroidery hoop. Lay it over the smaller ring, then put the larger ring over the top, trapping the fabric in between both rings. Screw it tight.

3 Lightly draw a honeycomb design in the middle of the fabric with a pencil, and write the words 'bee happy' above — practice writing the words on a piece of paper first.

4 Thread the tapestry needle with yellow wool and stitch over the honeycomb design using a straight stitch. Next, stitch the 'bee happy' words with white tapestry wool.

5 Finish off by stitching small stripy yellow and black wool bees with white wool wings around the yellow honeycomb. Turn the hoop over, trim the loose fabric with scissors and your picture is ready to display.

You will need

Sea creature fishing game

- 5 x A4 sheets of felt in yellow, coral, pink, blue and green
- Coloured felt scraps for fins and scales
- Matching threads
- Contrasting embroidery threads
- Toy stuffing
- Embroidery needle
- Scissors
- Seven 2cm magnetic bag clasps
- Small empty cotton reel
- Hot glue gun
- 50cm long bamboo cane
- Washi tape/ coloured paper
- Wool or colourful string

Have a whale of a time!

This fun fishing game, made from felt, will keep little ones entertained and happy for ages

To make each sea creature

1 Take a piece of brightly coloured A4 felt and fold in half. Photocopy the sea creature templates below at 250%, cut out and pin to the folded felt.

2 Sew each creature through the photocopy paper and following the line of the template all the way around the edge. It helps to start sewing on a straight part of the template, not a tail or a claw. Remember to leave a 2-3cm gap for stuffing and three gaps on the crab for stuffing the body and two claws. Carefully tear away the paper template and make sure to remove any bits of paper that are caught in the stitches. Trim the seam allowance to 3mm.

3 Insert the magnetic eyes by deciding where you would like them to go and then cutting two small slits in the felt to feed the clasp of the eyes through. Each bag clasp comes with two pieces and two small metal circles to help secure them. For the eye, use the main part of the bag clasp that looks the most eye-like (ours have a depression that looks like a pupil). Carefully insert your fingers into the hole in the seam and manipulate the clasps so they are secure.

4 Next, place a little toy stuffing into the cavity of the creature. Don't try and stuff their extremities, such as the tails, as they look much cuter when only their tummies are full and puffy! Remember to stuff both of the crab claws, though.

5 Push the stuffing to one side so it's easier to get the creature under your sewing machine's foot and then sew the openings closed.

6 When you have made all five basic shapes, hand-sew the fins and scales in place, using a contrasting embroidery thread. To make the seahorse's mane, cut two felt rectangles, one 15 x 2cm and one 15 x 1cm. Place the smaller rectangle on top of the larger one and sew a medium-size running stitch along one edge. Gently pull the thread to gather the mane and give it a frilled look. Hand-sew the mane in place to the seahorse.

7 Decorate each creature with simple embroidery patterns — we've used stars and French knots. Then sew small smiles onto each creature.

To make the fishing rod

1 Take the empty cotton reel and thread onto a 40cm length of wool or string. Tie a knot in one end and then secure the cotton reel to the string by filling the base of the reel with hot glue from a glue gun.

2 While the glue is still hot, take the other half of one of the bag clasps and push it into the glue, so it sits flush with the base of the reel. Leave to dry.

3 Take the bamboo cane and decorate it with coloured washi tape or strips of coloured paper. Finally, tie the string to one end of the cane and secure with a piece of tape.

Sea creature templates

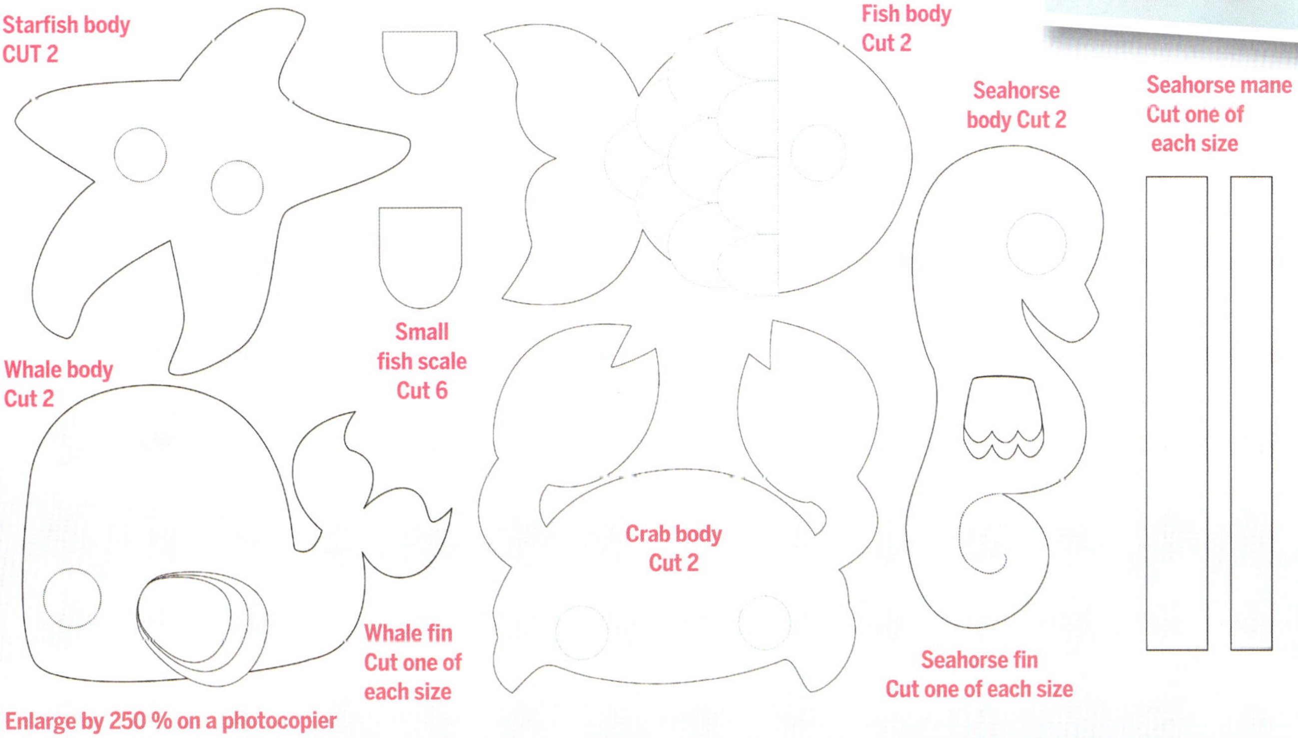

Make: Christine Leech. Photos: Barry Marsden.

You will need

Floral skirt

- Template
- Dressmaker's carbon paper & pencil
- Denim skirt
- Embroidery thread & needle
- Your basic sewing kit

Floral template

Photocopy or trace and then use dressmaker's carbon paper to transfer the design onto your fabric

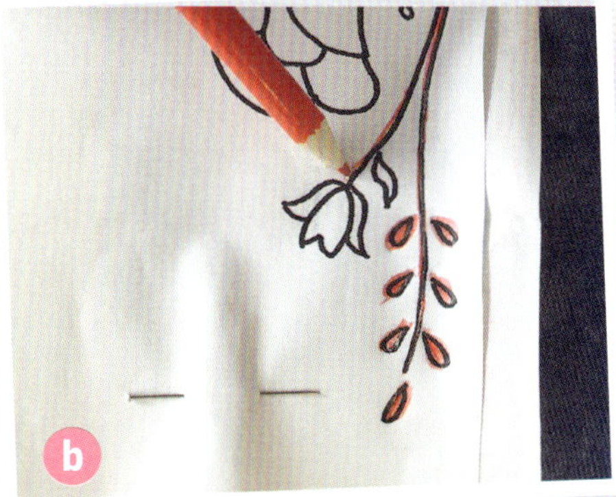

Floral skirt

Stitch our floral design onto practical denim and work the look

1 Photocopy the floral template above. Lay the carbon paper over the corner of the skirt and put the template on top (a). Trace the design onto the skirt with a pencil (b), leaving a carbon copy on the denim. If the design is faded, go over it with a vanishing marker.

2 With embroidery thread, start by sewing satin-stitch petals in pink, red and blue (c). Tie a knot on the reverse of your denim skirt to secure. Work groups of stitches in opposite directions to show the individual petals.

3 Within the centre of the satin-stitch flowers and over the dots in the pattern, work a series of French knots.

4 For the stems, use stem stitch. The longest stem is worked in threaded running stitch — stitch a running stitch then change to another thread, bring the needle up through the first running stitch and then weave the thread underneath the running stitches on alternate sides. Lazy-daisy stitch the looped leaves.

5 Repeat the pattern on the other side of the skirt using a mirrored photocopy of the template. Press skirt lightly on the reverse (d).

SONGSTER
NEEDLES
SHEFFIELD
ANCHOR
0237
FAST COLOUR
TREBLE
66
54
52

50

The Next Step

Take things a little further with these intermediate projects

76

Great Scott!

Bring some joy to a dog-lover's life with this adorable Scottish Terrier cushion

You will need

Scottie dog cushion

- 45 x 63cm blue ticking cotton canvas fabric
- 45 x 45cm cream cotton canvas fabric
- Large blue button
- Matching sewing thread
- Blue embroidery thread
- Large blue button
- Iron-on pattern pencil
- Tracing paper
- Embroidery needle
- Embroidery hoop
- 43cm-square cushion pad

To make

1 From the blue ticking fabric, cut two 31.5 x 45cm rectangles. Turn one of the long edges on each rectangle under by 1cm and then another 1cm. Pin and top stitch in a matching thread to secure.

2 Along the long edge of one of the rectangle pieces, stitch a buttonhole in the centre that's large enough for your blue button.

3 Photocopy the Scottie dog template (below) at 140% and trace over the top of the motif with an iron-on pattern pencil and tracing paper. Turn the tracing over and position in the centre on the right hand side of the cream cotton square. Using a hot iron without steam, press and hold the tracing over the fabric until the image has been transferred.

4 Place the piece of fabric inside an embroidery hoop with the design in the middle. Using three strands of blue embroidery thread, back stitch over all the individual lines left by the transfer pencil.

5 Once the Scottie dog has been embroidered, remove your work from the hoop and press.

6 Pin the two ticking rectangles to the embroidered square with right sides facing so that the rectangles overlap. Make sure that the buttonholed rectangle is stacked with the other striped rectangle on top of it. Sew all the way around the edge with a 1.5cm seam allowance. Turn right sides out and press. Where the buttonhole overlaps the other piece of backing fabric, position the button and sew it securely in place. Stuff the cover with a cushion pad.

TOP TIP If denim blue doesn't fit with your colour scheme, opt for a neutral grey ticking, a traditional red or a bold pop of pink.

Scottie Dog template

Enlarge by 140% on a photocopier

Words: Esme Clemo. Photo: Barry Marsden

Birds of paradise

Bright and bold, this fiesta-style embroidered tote bag is perfect for shopping in the sunshine

You will need

Tote bag
Finished size: 32 x 38cm

- Pink cotton fabric
- Patterned fabric scraps
- Paper-backed fusible web
- Embroidery thread in yellow and green
- Embroidery needle
- Matching thread
- Scissors
- Pins
- Sewing machine
- Tracing paper
- Iron-on transfer pencil

Template

Enlarge by 220% on a photocopier

1 For the front and back, cut out two rectangles from the pink fabric, measuring 35 x 43cm. For the handles, cut out two strips measuring 8 x 50cm.

2 Enlarge the template by 220%. Using a piece of tracing paper and transfer pencil, copy the template onto the bag front, using an iron on a low heat setting.

3 For the bird and leaf appliqués, transfer the two bird and leaf outlines onto the paper backing of the fusible web. Adhere them to the backs of the patterned fabric scraps and cut them out.

4 Remove the paper backings and, using the transfer pencil lines as a guide, position the birds on the bag front. Fuse in place following the maker's instructions.

5 Following the transfer pencil lines, embroider over the markings. Use our photo (right) as a guide for what colours to use. For the bird outlines, tree trunk and twigs, use stem stitch. For the sun, leaves and bird details, use back stitch. Add French knots to the tail ends on the bird.

6 Once stitched, press the bag front to smooth out any creases. Pin the bag pieces right sides together with edges aligned. Sew all the way around the edge with a 1.5cm seam allowance, making sure to leave the top edge open.

7 Turn the top edge of the bag under by 1.5cm and then a further 2.5cm. Stitch in place as close to the folded edge as possible.

8 To make the handles, turn the long sides under by 1cm on both strips. Fold the strips in half lengthways and pin them, then topstitch along the folded edge.

9 Measure 10cm in from either side of the bag and use a pin to mark these measurements. Pin the ends of each handle to the inside of the bag at these markings, make sure that the handles are at least 3cm inside the bag. Secure by top stitching a robust crossed square at all of the handle ends.

TOP TIP

If you prefer subtler shades, try making yours in greys and blues for a cooler look.

Hooting marvellous

A merry woodland creature that's perfect for the young ones in your life, or even just as a decoration for your home

You will need

Finished size: 19 x 22cm

- Tracing paper and pencil
- Two 30cm squares of teal felt
- 10 x 5cm rectangle of coral felt
- 15cm square of mustard felt
- 10cm square of bonding web
- 30cm square of light turquoise felt
- Crewel embroidery needle
- Purple and light turquoise stranded cotton embroidery thread
- Air-erasable fabric pen
- Matching sewing threads
- Polyester toy filling

Making paper patterns

On a photocopier, enlarge the templates by 200%, or so that each square measures 2.5cm. Trace the patterns onto tracing paper, placing the base on folded tracing paper, matching the fold line to the fold. Mark the notches, dots and details. Cut out the patterns and open out flat.

Cutting out

You will need one pair of owl bodies and one base from teal felt. Snip the notches and mark the dots on the wrong side of the pieces with a pencil. Trace two circles and one beak onto the paper backing of the bonding web. Roughly cut out the pieces, leaving a margin around each piece and press the circles on to the coral felt and the beak on to the mustard felt. Cut out the circles and beak.

Making the owl

Note: Take a 6mm seam allowance throughout. Join pieces with right sides together and edges level.

1 Peel the backing papers off the circles and beak. Arrange the pieces on the right side of one body panel; this will be the front of the owl. Press the pieces in place. Stitch close to the outer edges of the circles and beak. Draw eyes on the right side of the circles with a sharp HB pencil. Use a crewel embroidery needle and three strands of purple stranded cotton to embroider the eyes with straight stitches.

2 Pierce the ends of the lines for the feathers on the body pattern with a pin. Place the pattern on the front body panel and dot through the holes with an air-erasable fabric pen. Use a crewel embroidery needle and three strands of light turquoise stranded cotton to embroider the feathers with single fly stitches.

3 Draw one pair of feet on mustard felt with an air-erasable fabric pen. Pin another layer of mustard felt underneath. Carefully stitch along the drawn lines, leaving the short straight edges open. Carefully cut out the feet, cutting just outside the stitching. Pin and tack the feet to the front owl matching points A and B.

4 Draw one pair of wings on light turquoise felt with an air-erasable fabric pen. Pin another layer of light turquoise felt underneath. Carefully stitch along the drawn lines, leaving the notched edges open. Carefully cut out the wings, cutting just outside the stitching. Tack the notched edges. Pin and tack the wings to the front owl matching points C and D and the notches. Stitch one wing to the owl.

5 Pin and stitch the body panels together E-D-C-C-D-E, leaving a gap where one wing has been stitched to the main body. Clip the corners and snip the curves then finger press the seam open. Pin and stitch the body to the base E-A-B-B-A-E-A-B-B-A-E. Snip the curves then turn the owl right side out. Stuff the body firmly. Slip stitch the gap closed.

Finger pressing

Intricate seams are usually too difficult to press open on small items, so open the seam and run a moistened finger along it. Leave fabric to dry before handling the owl.

Owl template

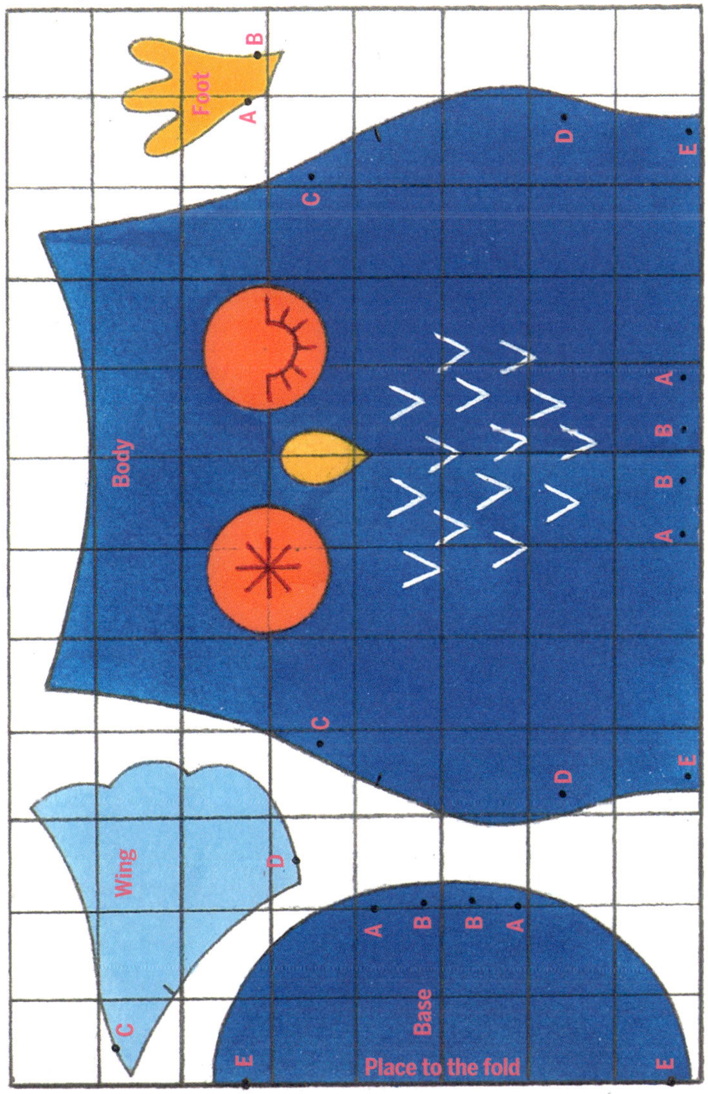

Enlarge by 200% on a photocopier

Make: Cheryl Cwen. Photo: Barry Marsden. Illustration: Terry Evans

The cactus club

A gorgeous cushion design which will brighten up any room in your home

You will need

Cactus cushions

- 1m x 105cm white cotton
- Stuffing or three 30 x 30cm square cushion pads
- 33 x 93cm low loft batting
- Paper-backed fusible web
- 10 x 35cm terracotta cotton
- 6 x 10cm pink cotton
- Four 12 x 12cm pieces of different green-patterned cotton
- Small scrap of floral fabric
- Matching sewing thread
- Hand-sewing needle
- Three 30cm white zips
- Sewing machine
- Zipper foot
- Even-feed quilting foot with quilter guide
- Seam ripper
- Scissors
- Cactus templates (opposite page) enlarged by 375%

Cutting out

1 For the cushion fronts, cut six 33 x 33cm squares from the white cotton and three 33 x 33cm squares from the batting.

2 For the cushion backs, cut three 13 x 33 cm rectangles and three 23 x 33cm rectangles from the white cotton.

3 For the appliqués, press the fusible web to the wrong side of the coloured and floral cottons. Using the templates, cut out three plant pots from the terracotta cotton and three plant-pot rims from the pink cotton. For the cacti, cut out the basic shape of each plant from three of the green cottons. Then cut out individual sections of each cactus from the fabric using our photo as a guide. Cut out four flowers from the floral fabric.

TOP TIP

Add texture to the plain background with some easy quilting techniques.

Templates

Enlarge by 375% on a photocopier

Instructions

1 Take a pair of cushion backs, one 13 x 33cm rectangle and one 23 x 33cm rectangle, and pin them together along one long side. Mark the first and last 5cm along the side. Sew the first 5cm with a regular straight stitch, and then the next 23cm with a long tacking stitch, and finish with another regular straight stitch for the last 5cm.

2 Press seam open. Position zip in the centre of the tacked line of stitches with the pull-tab butting against the regular straight stitches. Pin zip in place.

3 Using a zipper foot, stitch about 1cm all the way around the zip to secure. Cut the tacked seam open with a seam ripper and pull out the threads to reveal the zip beneath. Repeat for the other cushion backs.

4 To make the appliqués, layer the cut-out cactus pieces over the basic cactus shapes and press to fuse them together.

5 Take one cushion front and arrange the appliqué pieces in the centre, using our photo as a guide. Fuse in place with an iron.

6 Sandwich a piece of batting between two of the cushion fronts, with the appliqué cushion front on top and wrong sides facing. Pin the layers together and then quilt in your preferred style using a quilting foot. Make sure to stitch the appliqué to secure, and repeat for the other cushions.

7 To sew the cushion together, pin the front and back cushion pieces together with edges aligned. Make sure the zipper is open, ready for turning. Sew all the way around the edge, clip the corners and turn right sides out.

8 Stuff with a small cushion pad or fill with stuffing if you prefer. Repeat with the other two cushions.

Stitching for the kitchen

Cross stitch these pretty kitchen projects using the squares on gingham fabric

Oven glove

You will need

Oven glove

- 35cm of 112cm-wide gingham fabric
- 35cm x 50cm cotton wadding
- 35 x 50cm insulated lining
- Matching cotton thread
- Pinking shears
- Red bias binding
- Embroidery hoop
- Red embroidery thread
- White embroidery thread
- Cross stitch needle
- Embroidery scissors

Cutting out

Enlarge the template (right) by 350% and cut out two glove shapes from the fabric, wadding and lining with pinking shears. Turn the template over and cut out another two reverse glove shapes from the fabric.

Cross-stitching the fabric

1 Take one of the gingham fabric cutouts and place in the embroidery hoop.

2 Following the cross stitch chart (above) as a guide, use two strands of white and then red embroidery thread in your needle to work the cross stitches in the design, 4cm from the cuff edge. To work the loops linking the cross stitches, bring the needle through to the front of the work at A (see the illustrations below), loop underneath the red stitch at B and return to the reverse of the work at A. Repeat for the rest of the pattern.

Oven glove & tea towel cross stitch chart

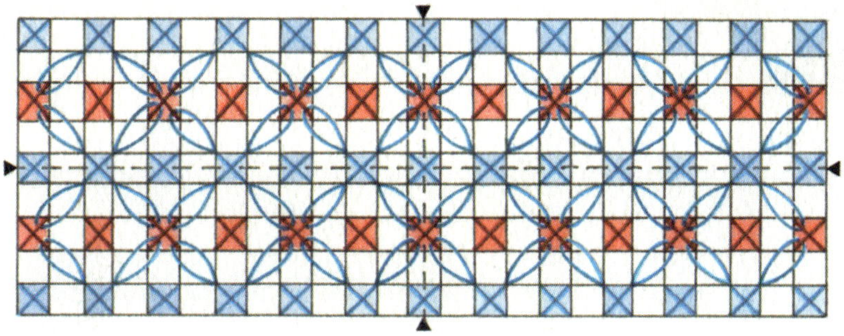

Oven glove template

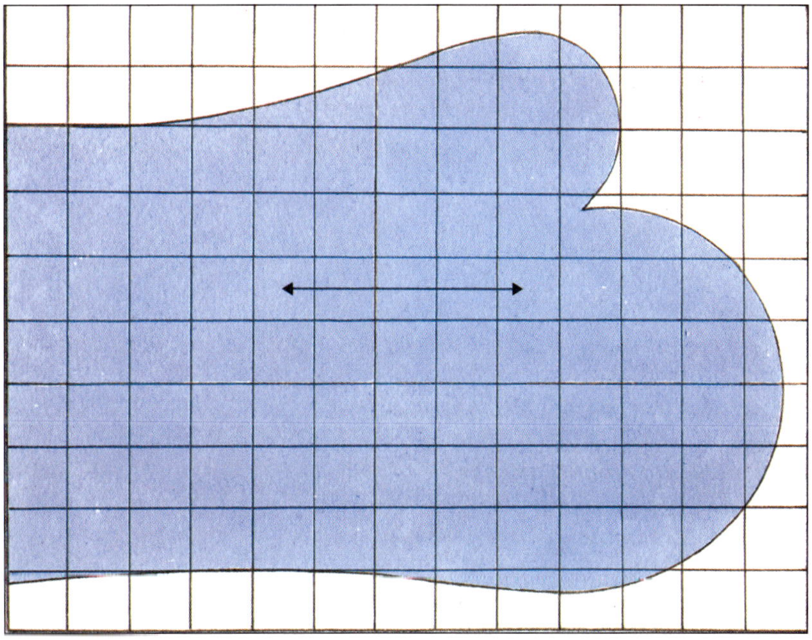

Enlarge by 350% on a photocopier

Making the glove

1 Place the cotton wadding on the wrong side of one of the reverse gingham cutouts, followed by the insulated lining and the cross-stitched gingham cutout. Repeat for the other pieces to create a sandwich. Pin and tack around the edges.

2 With a 1cm seam allowance, stitch the edges and leave the cuff open. Trim the seam allowance to reduce bulk and press the seams open at the cuff.

3 Open out the bias binding and pin to the raw edge of the cuff. Remove the bed of the sewing machine and slip the glove cuff under the needle. Stitch the binding in place with a 1cm seam allowance.

4 Turn the glove right sides out. Turn the binding over the cuff's raw edge and pin in place. Top stitch close to the binding's pressed edge and slip stitch where the binding overlaps.

How to work the stitches

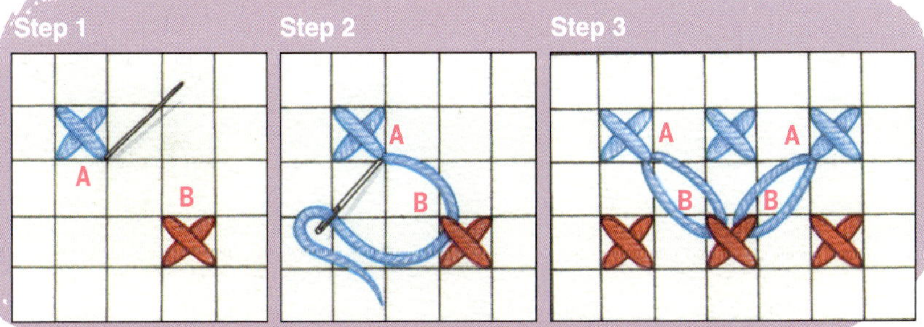

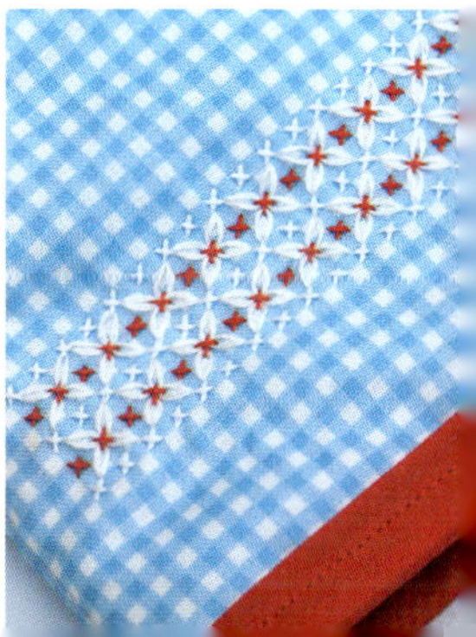

Makes and styling: Esme Clemo. Photos: Barry Mersden. Illustrations: Terry Evans

Tea towel

You will need

Tea towel

- 10 x 60cm gingham fabric
- Matching cotton thread
- Fabric scissors
- 120cm red ric rac
- Embroidery hoop
- Red embroidery thread
- White embroidery thread
- Cross stitch needle
- Embroidery scissors
- 50 x 70cm white tea towel

Cross stitching the fabric

1 Place the gingham fabric in the embroidery hoop. Following the chart on page 57 as a guide, stitch across four gingham squares for every square on the chart to enlarge the design.

2 Work the cross stitches using two strands of red and white embroidery thread, and the loops with two strands of white embroidery thread to copy across the design.

Sewing the trim to the tea towel

1 Fold and press the edges of the cross-stitched gingham under by 1cm.

2 Pin the ric rac to the hemmed long edges of the gingham and then pin the trim to one end of the tea towel. Fold the extra lengths round to the reverse of the tea towel and fold under the open ends. Pin in place.

3 Top stitch close to the edge of the gingham in matching thread, securing the cross-stitched trim in place.

4 Slip stitch the open seams on the reverse of the tea towel closed.

Bowl cover

You will need

Bowl cover

- Circle of gingham fabric (measuring 5cm wider than the bowl you want to cover)
- Matching cotton thread
- Fabric scissors
- Red bias binding
- Thin elastic
- Safety pin or bodkin
- Embroidery hoop
- Red embroidery thread
- White embroidery thread
- Cross-stitch needle
- Embroidery scissors

Cutting out

Using the bowl you wish to cover as a guide, cut a circle out of your fabric that measures 5cm wider than the rim of your bowl.

Cross-stitching the fabric

Place the gingham fabric in the embroidery hoop. Following the teapot chart (below) as a guide, use two strands of red embroidery thread for the teapot and cups, and two strands of white embroidery thread to cross stitch the steam design.

Making the cover

1 Pin and top stitch the bias binding around the raw edge of the circle of fabric, leaving an opening where the two ends meet.

2 Measure around your bowl and subtract 5cm to work out how much elastic you will need.

3 Thread the elastic onto the safety pin or bodkin to guide the elastic around the binding and stitch the ends together to secure.

4 Slip stitch the bias binding opening closed and place the fabric cover over your bowl.

Bowl cover cross stitch chart

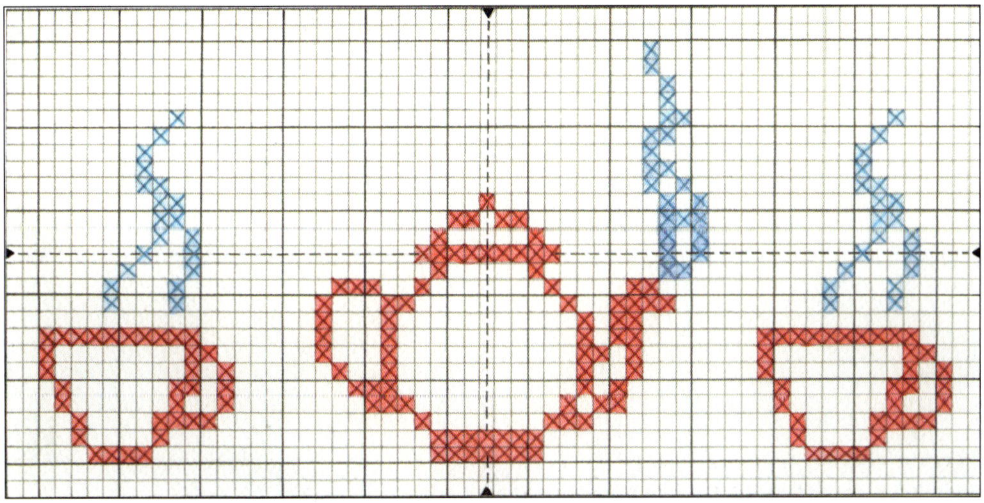

TOP TIP

When your cross stitch is complete, remove from the hoop and press it lightly on the wrong side.

Snap happy

Use special family photos to create these gorgeous makes for your home

You will need

Family in a frame

- A white box frame
- Linen fabric
- Lightweight iron-on interfacing
- Photo
- Thick card
- Thin card
- Red and black stranded embroidery thread
- Cutting board
- Pencil
- Metal ruler
- Craft knife
- Screwdriver (optional)
- Paintbrush (optional)
- Fade-away marker pen
- Scissors
- Embroidery needle
- Masking tape
- Fabric glue
- Staple gun

a

b

c

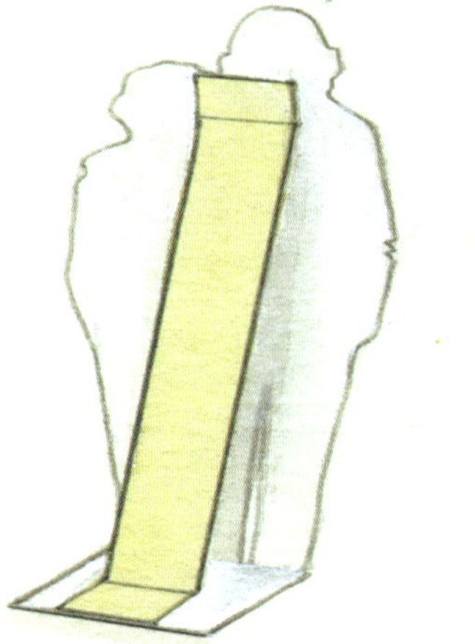

d

1 Remove the back of the box frame using a screwdriver to lever out staples, if needed. Place the back on to the thick card on the cutting board, mark around it in pencil, then cut out using the metal ruler and craft knife.

2 Using the thick card as a template, cut out a piece of linen and interfacing, adding a 1.5cm seam allowance around all edges. Press interfacing to wrong side of linen, following manufacturer's instructions.

3 Using your photo as a guide, draw a rough version of its background as an outline on to the linen fabric using the fade-away marker pen (a). Leave the upper section of the linen clear.

4 Cut out the figure(s) from the photo, leaving a 1.5cm tab along the lower edge. Lay the figure on to the drawn background and write their name in the space above, using the fade-away marker pen (b).

5 Using three strands of embroidery thread; embroider the background in black, using varying sizes of straight stitch and back stitch — you don't have to be too precise. Embroider the name in red using chain stitch. Press flat.

6 Lay the cloth on a flat surface with interfacing uppermost. Place thick card on top, fold over hem edges and stick down with masking tape (c). Place embroidery into back of frame, then secure backing using a staple gun.

7 Fold under tab on base of figure. Cut a narrow strip of thin card to same height of figure, plus 1.5cm. Fold over strip ends. Stick figure to base of frame, then stick folded ends of strip to back of figure and base of frame to make a triangular support (d). Leave to dry.

Feature: Jan Dabbous and Jane Bolsover. Photos: Delphine Adburgham. Illustrations: Terry Evans

TOP TIP

Don't worry if you get glue on the outside of the metal frame — it's easy to scrape off.

Spring blooms

Inspired by the ever-popular tulip, cross stitch this beautiful floral design and make a cushion

You will need

Spring bloom cushion

- 50cm of 140cm-wide 35-count linen fabric in Pale Rose
- 1 skein of Anchor stranded cotton embroidery thread in 254 (Lime green), 240 (Mid green), 264 (Light green), 140 (Mid blue), 160 (Light blue), 36 (Mid pink) and 10 (Light pink)
- Size 28 tapestry needle
- Matching sewing thread
- 40cm square cushion pad

Design Chart & Stitch Guide

Key:

- 254 (Lime green)
- 264 (Light green)
- 160 (Light blue)
- 10 (Light pink)
- 240 (Mid green)
- 140 (Mid blue)
- 36 (Mid pink)

Embroidering cross stitch

Each cross stitch is taken over four threads of the fabric, using three strands of embroidery thread in the needle. Each square on the chart represents 4 x 4 threads of the fabric.

Bring the needle to the right side at the upper-left corner and insert it four threads down and four threads to the right, forming a diagonal stitch. Bring the needle to the right side, four threads up.

To complete an individual stitch, insert the needle four threads down and four threads to the left, thereby making a diagonal stitch.

Alternatively, continue to make a row of half-stitches then work back, completing the upper half of the crosses.

Bands of stitching line the top and bottom of the cushion

Embroidering the cross stitch front

1 Cut out a square of linen measuring 50 x 50cm.

2 Measure 5.5cm in from the left-hand edge and 11.5cm down from the top edge. Start embroidering one band of flowers, copying the chart. When you have completed the stitches on the chart, repeat to continue across the fabric a total of four times, then stitch the chart as far as the red line.

3 Turn the fabric so the cross-stitched band is horizontal across the bottom. Repeat step 2. When complete, press the work face down on a towel. Trim 3.5cm from all edges of the fabric, leaving a 43 x 43cm square.

Making the cushion

1 Cut two 29 x 42cm rectangles for the back from linen. Press under 1cm, then 1.5cm on one long edge of each back piece. Stitch close to the inner pressed edges to hem the pieces.

2 With the outer edges level and right sides together, pin the backs to the cushion front, overlapping the hemmed edges. Stitch the outer edges with a 1.5cm seam allowance. Clip the corners, turn right side out and insert the cushion pad.

12
1
2
3
4
5
6
7
8
9
10
11
12
1
2
3
4
5
6
7
8
9
10
11

A stitch in time!

Make telling the time fun with these children's cat and dog clocks

You will need

For each clock

- Vanishing fabric marker
- Matching cotton thread
- 6in embroidery hoop
- Embroidery thread in dark brown, lime green, bright pink, mustard yellow, purple, light blue, magenta, dark green, navy, bright yellow, lilac, red, blue and yellow
- Scissors
- Embroidery scissors
- Embroidery needle
- Hand sewing needle
- Clock quartz movement and clock hands
- Yellow or green spray paint
- Pink or turquoise ribbon
- Thick cardboard

Ear templates

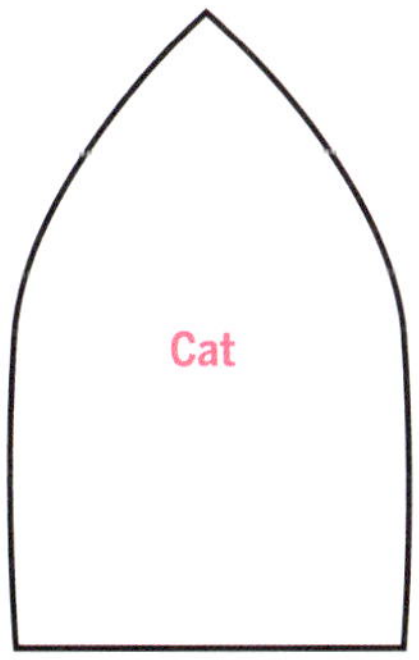

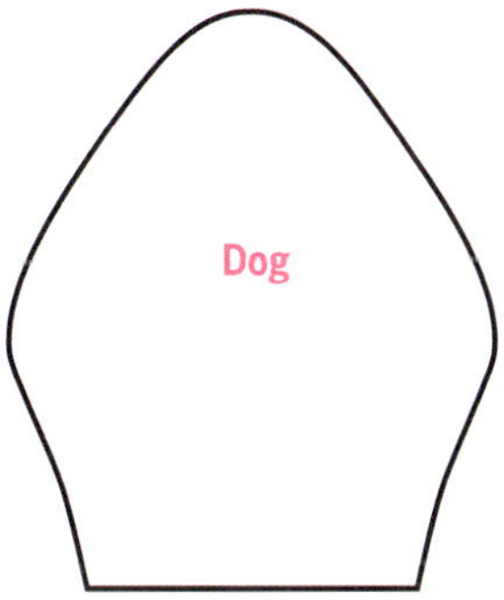

Enlarge by 200% on a photocopier

Making the ears

Enlarge the ear templates by 200% and cut out four ears for each clock from the fabric. Pin two cutouts right sides together and machine sew with a 1cm seam allowance, leaving the bottoms open. Turn right sides out and repeat to create a pair of ears.

For the cat, sew a running stitch around the edge with two strands of green embroidery thread and press.

For the dog, fold the ear tips down and press in place.

Making the template

Photocopy our photo of the clock face and enlarge it so it measures 20cm across. Trace the embroidery design and centre of the clock hands on to your fabric using a vanishing fabric marker.

Embroidering the fabric

1 Place the fabric within the embroidery hoop and stitch the traced numbers in chain stitch for the cat or stem stitch for the dog, using two strands of embroidery thread. For each number, use a different colour of embroidery thread.

2 To stitch the animal faces, use two strands of dark brown embroidery thread to satin stitch the nose and eyes, and back stitch a mouth and cat's whiskers. For the dog's cheeks, use four strands to create the French knots.

3 Remove the fabric from the embroidery hoop and press lightly on the reverse.

Painting the hoop and the clock hands

1 Working in a well-ventilated area, spray the outer embroidery hoop and clock hands in yellow for the dog and green for the cat. Apply a few thin coats, and wait for each coat to dry completely before you begin to apply the next one.

2 Allow the hoop and hands to dry for 48 hours.

Making the clock

1 Draw around the inside of the inner embroidery hoop onto thick cardboard and cut out with scissors

2 Place the embroidered fabric in the hoop and tighten the screw.

3 Put the cardboard circle into the back of the embroidery hoop to sit against the fabric. Push a pin through the centre of the cardboard and clock face to mark the centre, enlarging the hole slightly with a pencil.

4 Push the clock's movement shaft through the back of the cardboard and fabric. Attach the clock hands to the front of the clock face, following the manufacturer's instructions.

5 Trim the excess fabric on the reverse of the embroidery hoop to 2.5cm. Using a handsewing needle and matching thread, sew a running stitch around the edge of the remaining fabric, pull taut and secure the thread end.

6 Position the ears on the reverse of the hoop and hand-sew to the excess fabric.

7 Loop a length of matching ribbon through the embroidery hoop screw, and use it to hang your clock.

TOP TIP

Blanket stitch a circle of felt to the reverse of the clock to neaten up the back, but don't forget to cut out a square for the clock movement so you can replace the batteries.

Makes: Esme Clemo. Photos: Sussie Bell.

Make: Jacqueline Dawe. Styling: Emily Dawe. Photos: Sussie Bell. Illustrations: Terry Evans

Sew tidy

Keep cottons, pins, scissors and other craft tools in easy reach with this practical and stylish organiser

You will need

Sew Tidy

- 150 x 100cm of medium-weight Calico fabric
- 44 x 20cm red and cream gingham fabric
- Small coat hanger
- Anchor embroidery threads in: 334 (Red), 239 (Green), 288 (Yellow), 111 (Purple) and 433 (Blue)
- 1.5cm-wide cotton ribbon
- Embroidery needle
- Matching sewing threads
- Fabric scissors
- Tracing paper
- Tape measure
- Pencil

From the Calico, cut:

Front and back: two pieces of fabric, 40cm wide (or 4cm wider than the coat hanger) and 50cm long.
Cotton-reel pockets: five 14 x 14cm squares.
Thimble pocket: one 7 x 7cm square
Using templates (page 69), cut two scissor pockets.

From the gingham, cut:

Two pieces 12 x 9cm and two pieces 10 x 10cm.

1 Lay the back panel right side down. Mark a vertical line at the centre-top edge. Draw a horizontal line about 15cm down from the top edge to help keep the coat hanger straight.

2 Place the coat hanger centrally, 1cm down from the top edge, draw around the top curve. This will be your seam line. Draw the curved shape again, 1cm up from the first line. Extend the line out to the side edges. Mark a 1cm gap at the centre top of the draw line, and cut around your marked shape. Cut the front panel to match.

3 Using tracing paper, transfer the motifs (on page 69) onto their respective pockets, positioning them in the middle. The cotton reels should be 4cm up from the bottom edge, the scissors 2cm up from the bottom edge, the thimble 1cm above the bottom edge.

4 For the outlines, work back stitch, using brown embroidery thread for the cotton reels and thimble, and dark red for the two pairs of scissors. For the cotton reels, work long stitches, close together, from one side to the other, using red, green, yellow, purple and blue embroidery threads. For the thimble and scissors, work dots on the thimble and scissors with short straight stitches or French knots.

5 Press a 2cm hem at the top of the cotton-reel pockets, pin a strip of ribbon along this edge and machine-stitch in place. Press a 0.5cm turning to the top edge of the scissors and thimble pockets, pin and machine-stitch a strip of ribbon to the top edge.

6 Press a 1cm turning along the two square pieces of gingham fabric and along the shorter edge of the remaining two gingham pieces. Pin and machine-stitch the ribbon along this edge.

7 For the cotton-reel and gingham pockets, press a 1cm turning along the side edges then fold back and press a similar turning along the bottom edge. Do the same with the thimble and scissor pockets using 0.5cm turnings.

8 Press a 1cm pleat each side of the cotton-reel pockets and a 0.5cm pleat to the sides of the thimble pocket to give them depth. Put a few stitches at the lower end of each pleat to hold in place. Tack a 1cm hem to the lower edge of the cotton-reel pockets and a 0.5cm hem to the thimble and scissor pockets, then press.

9 Arrange the pleated pockets along the front panel, 4cm up from the bottom edge, with the first and fifth pockets 3cm in from the sides. Pin and tack the pockets in place. Slip stitch the side and bottom edges to the front panel. Work a few stitches at each of the pocket corners to secure the multiple layers. Neaten the top inner seam allowance with a few stitches, then remove the tacking stitches.

10 Using our photos as a guide, position the scissor, thimble and gingham pockets in place. Pin and tack the pockets, then slip stitch the side and bottom edges of the scissor and thimble pockets, and machine-stitch the sides and lower edges of the gingham pockets. Remove all tacking stitches. Machine-stitch a length of ribbon across the lower edge of the front piece, 1.5cm from the lower edge.

11 With right sides facing, pin and tack the front and back pieces together, matching the corners. Machine-stitch along the curved seam line and down the side edges, leaving the bottom edge open and a 1cm gap in the top centre for the hanger to poke out.

12 Trim the corners and seam allowance by 0.5cm to remove any bulk. Press back the seam allowance then press under a 1cm hem around the open bottom edge. Turn right side out. Ease out the seam and press. Neaten the top opening with a few stitches and insert the coat hanger.

13 Finally, pin and tack the bottom front and back hems together, then neatly slip stitch together.

Pocket and motif templates

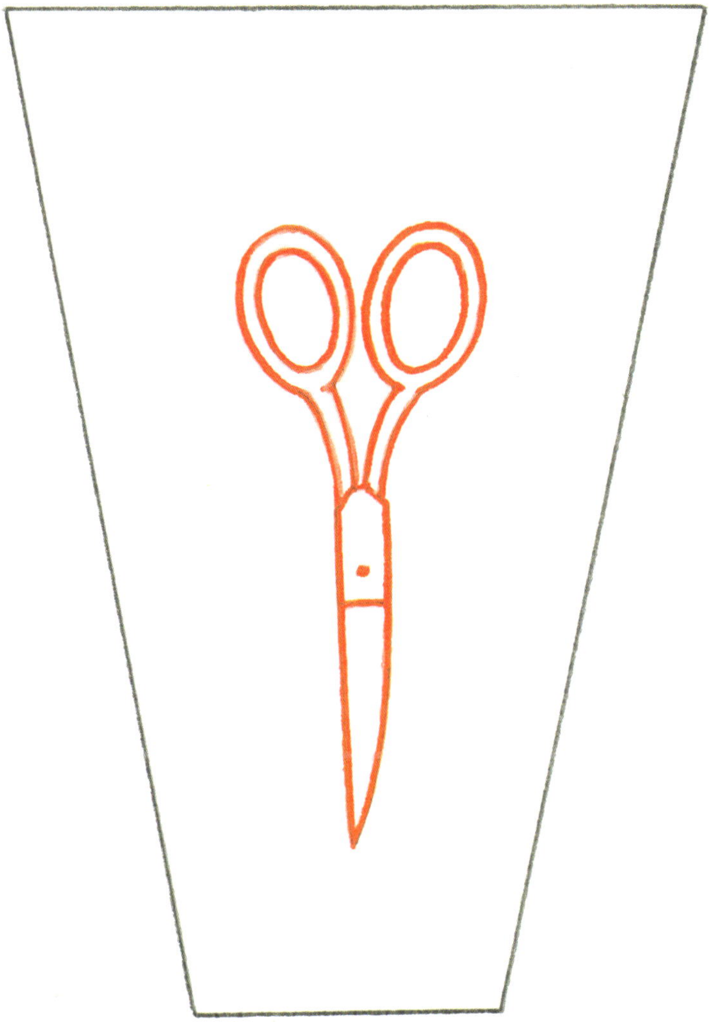

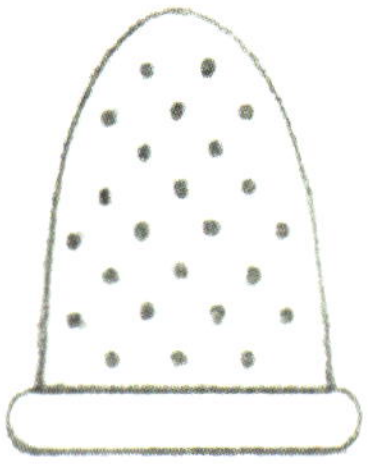

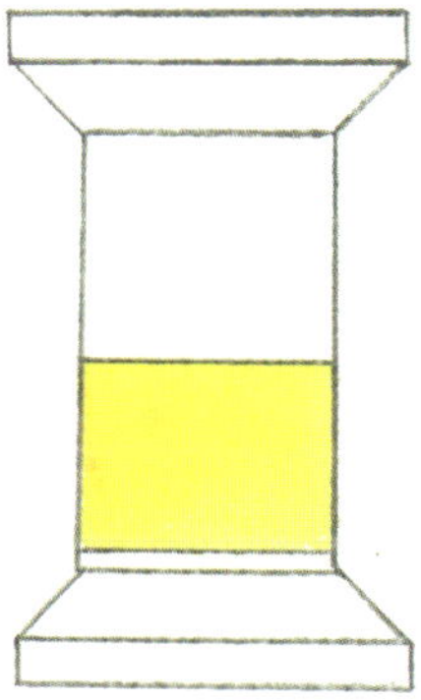

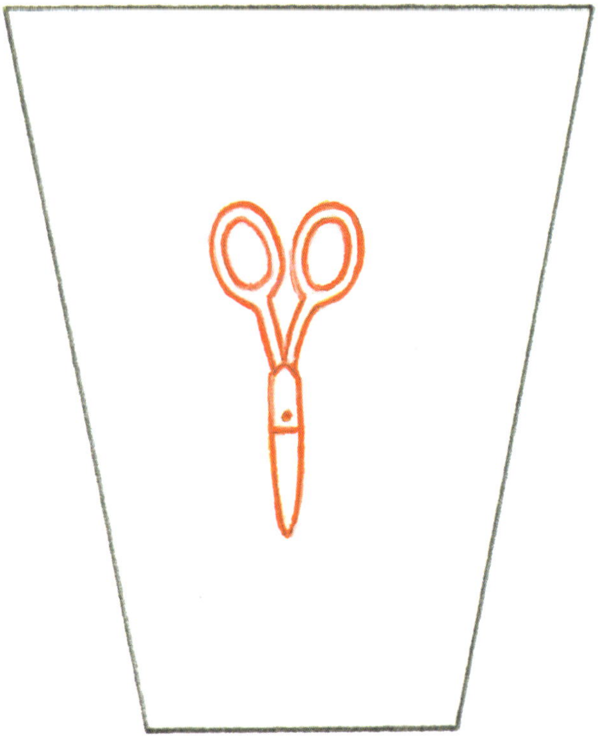

Shades of Autumn

Sew these four cross stitch designs to create a gorgeous seasonal picture

You will need

Finished size of each stitched motif approx: 6 x 6cm
Finished size of picture within our frame: 30 x 30cm

- 40 x 40cm piece of beige 28 count evenweave fabric (allowing for framing)
- DMC stranded embroidery cotton in the following colours: One skein each of 3819 (Yellow), 470 (Mid green), 3345 (Dark green), 680 (Bronze), 975 (Rust), 838 (Chestnut), 921 (Orange), 304 (Red) and 327 (Purple)
- Tapestry needle (size 24)
- Tacking thread
- 30cm embroidery hoop
- Picture frame with backing board, minimum aperture 30 x 30cm
- Ivory mount board, to fit frame
- Dressmaking pins
- Strong topstitching thread

Working the embroidery

1 Press the evenweave fabric, then mark the centre of your design by folding the fabric in half and then into quarters. Stitch two lines of tacking along the folds to form a central cross, worked through a row of holes in the fabric. Mount the fabric in the embroidery hoop with the tacking stitches centred.

2 The design is worked in cross stitch and back stitch. See our stitch guide, starting on page 10, for how to work the individual stitches. If you are a beginner, practise the stitches first on some spare evenweave fabric.

3 The charts on pagse 72-75 show the four individual motifs that make up our picture. You will need to work each of the smaller designs of our picture separately, while referring to the charts. Each coloured square represents one cross stitch worked over two threads of fabric, using two strands of embroidery thread in your needle. The solid lines represent back stitch, using one strand of embroidery thread in your needle. The key indicates the colour of thread used.

4 Starting at the centre of your design where the two tacking lines cross, count out seven fabric threads to the left of the vertical line and seven threads down from the horizontal line to find the top right-hand corner of the Acorn chart; mark position with a pin. Following the chart, stitch the Acorn motif.

5 Again, starting at the centre of the design where the two tacking lines cross, count out seven fabric threads to the right of the vertical line and seven threads down from the horizontal line to find the top left-hand corner of the Rose Hip chart; mark position with a pin. Following the chart, stitch the Rose Hip motif.

6 Repeat the counting process up to find the bottom right-hand corner of the Sycamore Key chart and the bottom left-hand corner of the Oak Leaf chart. Following the charts, stitch the Sycamore Key and Oak Leaf motifs.

7 When the embroideries are finished, remove tacking threads. Place work face down on a padded surface and press on the wrong side, under a damp cloth, using light pressure to avoid flattening the stitches.

Framing the embroideries

1 Remove the backing board from the frame. Centre the embroideries on backing board and use dressmaking pins along top edge to secure. Pull fabric firmly over lower edge and secure with more pins. Use strong top stitching thread to lace the fabric edges from top to bottom across the back of the board.

2 Repeat pinning with the side edges, pulling the fabric firmly until taut. Tuck under surplus fabric at corners and then lace from side to side across the back of the board. Remove the pins.

3 Cut mount board to fit frame and accurately mark the positions of the four motif windows. Cut out windows. Alternatively, take to a picture framers and ask them to cut the mount for you. Using a pencil, write the name of the embroidered specimen underneath each window. Place mount board and then embroidery into frame and secure in place at the back.

TOP TIP

For a slightly padded finish, cut a piece of felt or thin wadding to the size of the backboard. attach it using a spray glue suitable for fabric before lacing your embroidery to the board.

Sycamore key

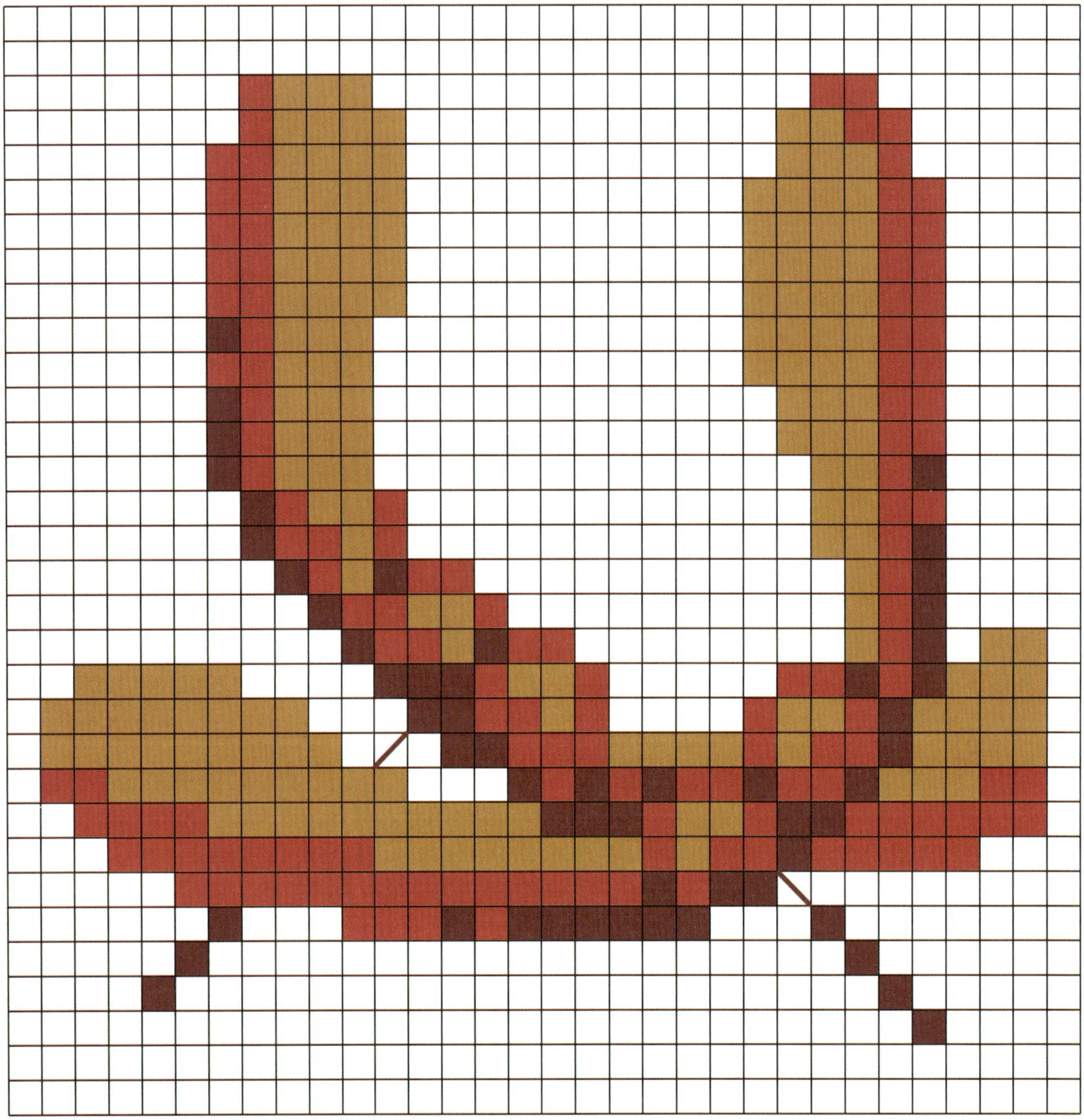

Cross stitch

Each coloured square represents one cross stitch worked with two strands of thread in the following colours:

- 680 (Bronze)
- 975 (Rust)
- 838 (Chestnut)

Back stitch

The solid lines represent back stitch worked with one strand of thread in the following colour:

- 838 (Chestnut)

Oak leaf

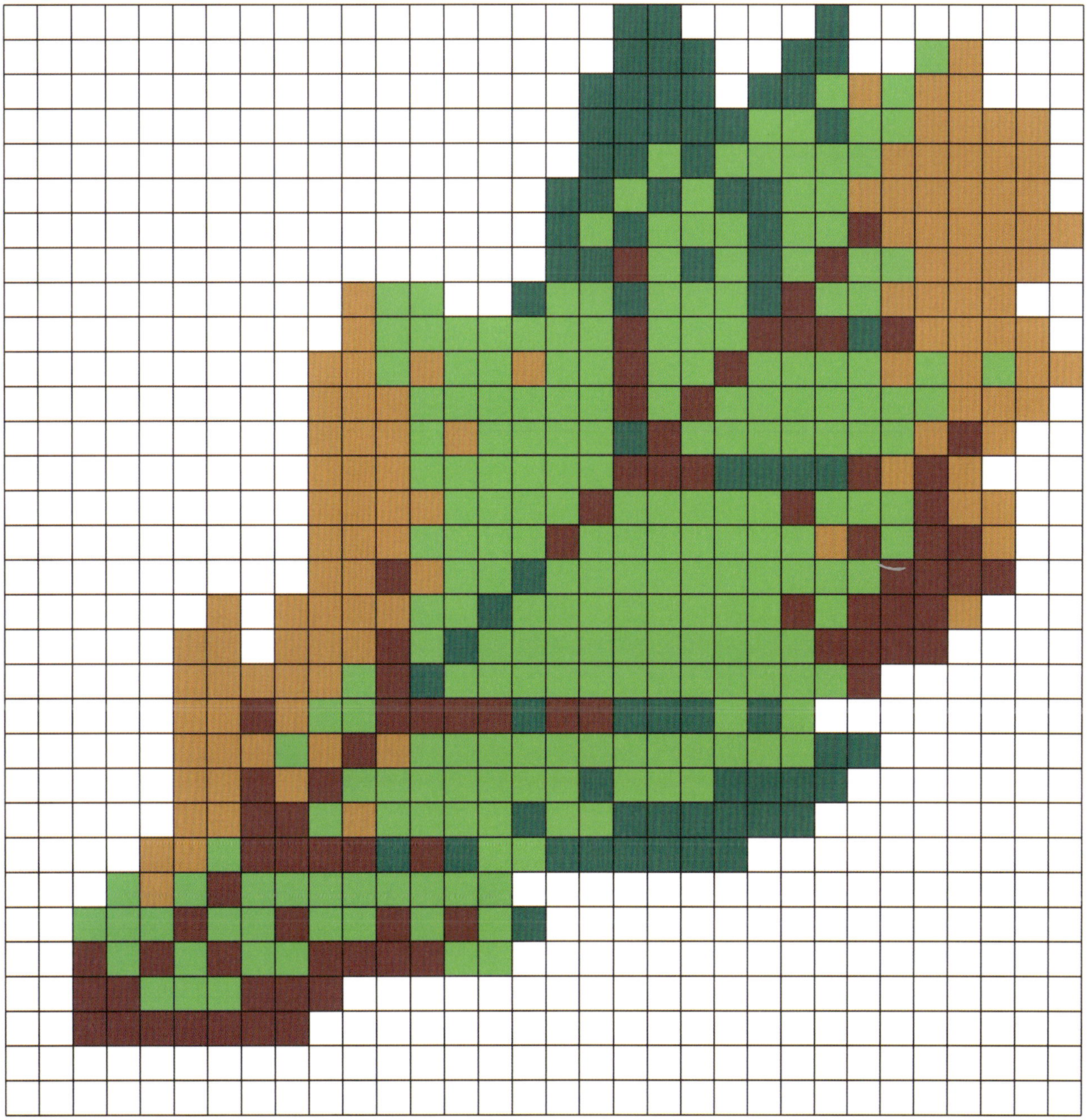

Cross stitch

Each coloured square represents one cross stitch worked with two strands of thread in the following colours:

- 470 (Mid green)
- 680 (Bronze)
- 3345 (Dark green)
- 838 (Chestnut)

Back stitch

The solid lines represent back stitch worked with one strand of thread in the following colour:

- 838 (Chestnut)

Acorn

Cross stitch

Each coloured square represents one cross stitch worked with two strands of thread in the following colours:

- 3819 (Yellow)
- 470 (Mid green)
- 3345 (Dark green)
- 680 (Bronze)
- 975 (Rust)

Back stitch

The solid lines represent back stitch worked with one strand of thread in the following colour:

- 838 (Chestnut)

Rose hip

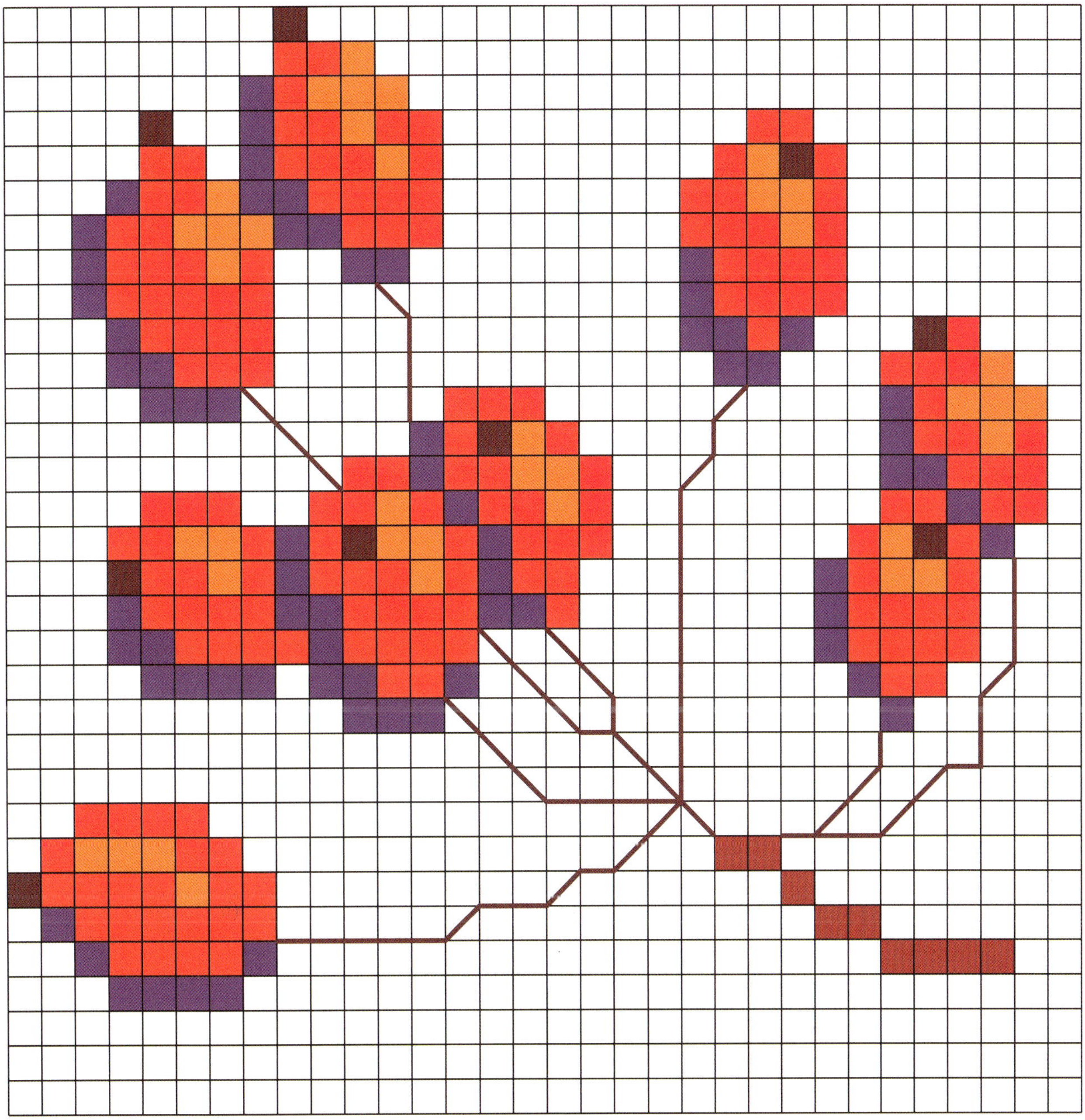

Cross stitch

Each coloured square represents one cross stitch worked with two strands of thread in the following colours:

- 975 (Rust)
- 304 (Red)
- 838 (Chestnut)
- 327 (Purple)
- 921 (Orange)

Back stitch

The solid lines represent back stitch worked with one strand of thread in the following colour:

- 838 (Chestnut)

Just coasting

When friends are popping over for a catch-up and a hot cuppa, make sure you have our fun coasters at the ready

You will need

For 4 Coasters

- 24 x 50cm piece of sand-coloured denim fabric
- 24 x 24cm piece of thin wadding Bondaweb
- 10 x 10cm pieces of cotton fabric in four different patterns
- Scissors
- Black and beige sewing threads

1 Cut out eight squares measuring 12 x 12cm from the sand-coloured fabric and four from the wadding. Fuse the Bondaweb to the wrong side of the patterned fabrics, using an iron and following the manufacturer's instructions.

2 Using our image as a guide, cut out coffee-cup shapes from the patterned fabric pieces. Remove the Bondaweb's paper backing from the fabrics and fuse the coffee-cup shapes to four of the sand-coloured squares.

3 Top stitch all the way around the cup motifs in the black sewing thread.

4 Put the squares into pairs with one appliquéd square matched with a plain square, making sure the right sides are facing. Place a piece of wadding on top and pin the layers together. Sew around three of the sides with a 1cm seam allowance. Clip corners and trim the seams. Turn right sides out and press.

5 Fold the raw edges inside the coasters by 1cm and pin together. Slip stitch the gaps closed and then top stitch in the beige sewing thread approximately 5mm from the edge.

Bee needlebook

Stitch this lovely busy, buzzy bee needle case following our step-by-step instructions

You will need

Bee needlebook

- Tracing paper
- Transfer pencil
- Embroidery hoop
- Embroidery thread in yellow, black and light grey
- Embroidery needle
- Embroidery scissors
- 13 x 20cm rectangle low-loft batting
- 20 x 26cm cream cotton fabric
- 17 x 20cm cream felt
- Matching sewing thread
- Hand-sewing needle
- Scissors

TOP TIP

Use the bee embroidery design to create a matching set of crafting accessories, like a pin cushion or scissor case.

1 Using the transfer pencil, trace the embroidery design from the template onto a piece of tracing paper. Place the tracing paper on the cotton fabric with tracing side down. With an iron set on low, press the paper to the fabric to transfer the design. Gently peel away the paper to reveal the embroidery design beneath.

2 Place the fabric in an embroidery hoop and tighten until taut. For the honeycomb design, work a series of straight stitches with two strands of yellow embroidery thread. This is the simplest stitch and can be worked to any length or direction. Bring the needle up through the fabric at the start of the line and take a single long stitch by inserting at the end of the line. Repeat until the entire honeycomb has been stitched.

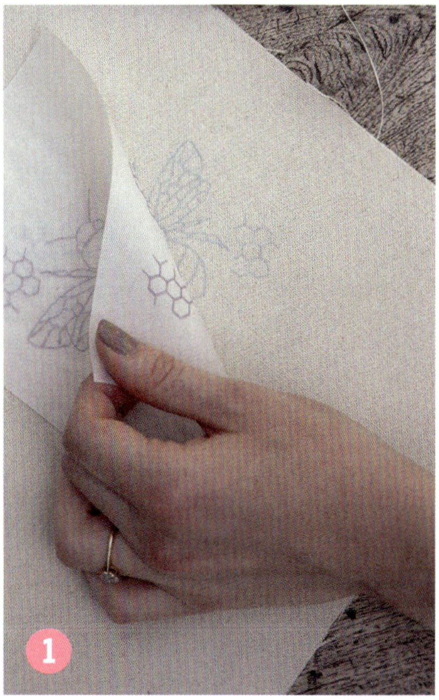

1

2

3 Using two strands of embroidery thread in black, back stitch over all the body and leg outlines left by the transfer pencil. Bring the needle up through to the right side of the fabric on the transfer line and make a single 2mm stitch backward. Then bring the tip of the needle up again, 2mm in front of its original entry hole, and draw the thread through. Take a another stitch backward, going down through the original entry hole and repeat to create a line of back stitches. Repeat in grey for the wings and antennae.

4 Fill in the design with a satin stitch in yellow, black and grey using our image as a guide. To satin stitch, work straight, parallel stitches closely together to cover the area; there should be no gaps between the stitches.

5 Remove the embroidery from the hoop and press to remove any creases. With the embroidery design positioned to the right, cut out a 13 x 20cm rectangle from the fabric for the needle-cover front. Cut out another rectangle to the same measurements for the back. Place the fabric pieces right sides together and top with the piece of batting. Pin and stitch all the way around the edge with a 5mm seam allowance, making sure to leave a 10cm gap on the bottom edge for turning through.

6 Turn right sides out and press. Turn the seam at the open gap inside the cover, pin and slip stitch the gap closed.

7 Position the felt insert inside the cover, with a 5mm gap all the way around. Place pin at the top and bottom edge to mark the centre and top stitch through the centre to secure in place.

8 Decorate the felt pages by adding some loops of ribbon and sewing on a button to help store your needles and thread.

Bee template

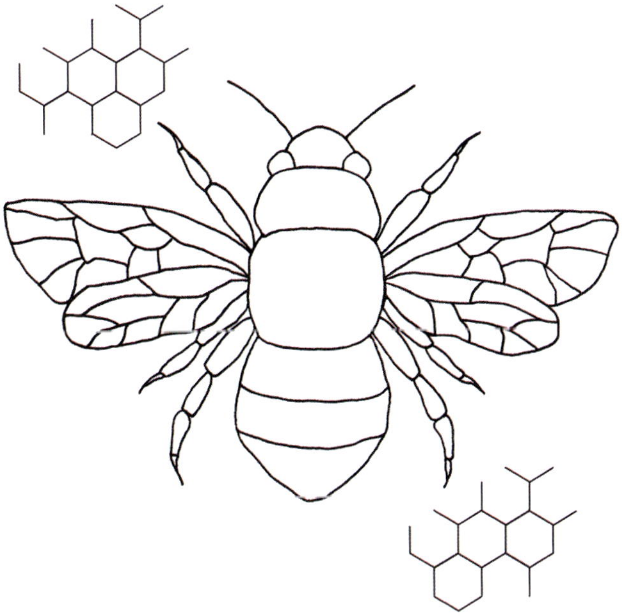

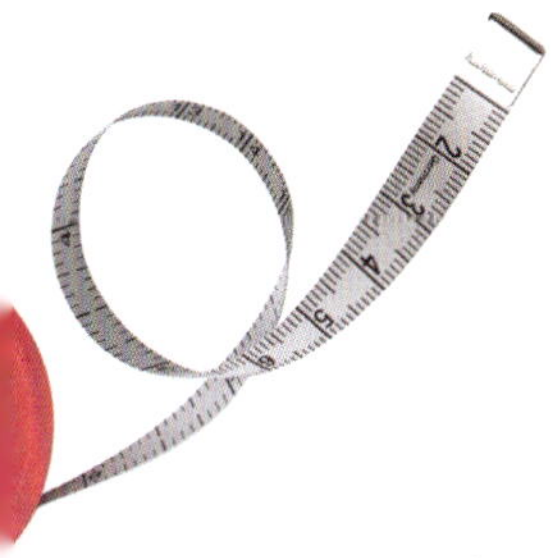

Fern cushion

Stitch this embroidered fern cushion in vibrant shades of orange and green

You will need

Finished size: 40 x 40cm

- Tracing paper and sharp HB pencil
- 1m of 110cm wide orange linen/cotton fabric
- Masking tape
- 43 x 43cm embroidery frame (stretcher)
- Three skeins of mid green and one skein of light green stranded cotton embroidery thread
- Three 2.2cm wooden buttons
- Matching sewing thread
- 40cm square cushion pad

Preparing the front

1 Cut a 50 x 50cm square of fabric, and draw a 43 x 43cm square centrally on the fabric for the front.

2 Tape the tracing right side up on the fabric, matching the broken line to one vertical drawn line with the cross 5cm above the lower horizontal drawn line. Redraw the fern to transfer the design to the fabric.

3 Remove the tracing and tape it to the fabric, matching the broken line to the other vertical drawn line with the cross 5cm below the upper horizontal drawn line. Redraw the fern to transfer the design to the fabric. Remove the tracing. Fix the front in the embroidery frame.

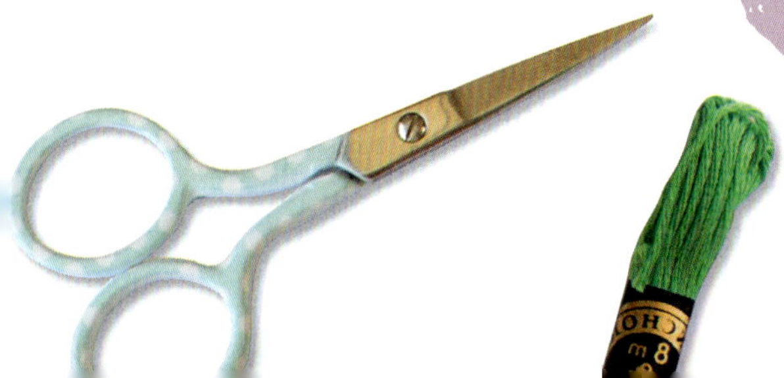

Fern template

On a photocopier, enlarge the template to 350%. Trace the fern, broken line and cross onto tracing paper. Redraw the fern on the wrong side of the tracing with a pencil.

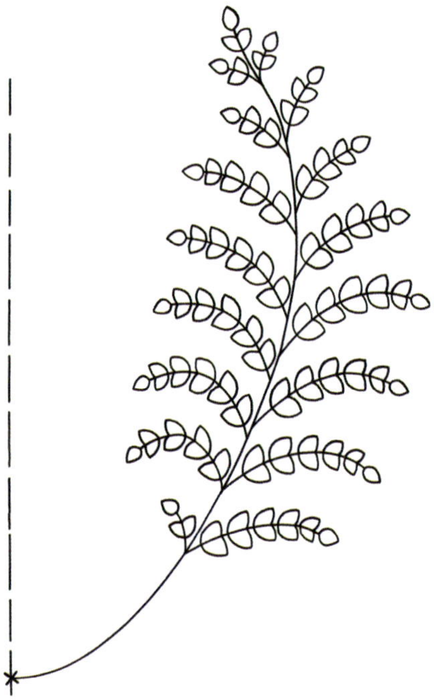

Embroidering the front

1 Use three strands of embroidery thread to embroider the leaves and stems. Embroider the leaflets in satin stitch using mid green embroidery thread. Embroider the stems in stem stitch using light green embroidery thread.

2 Remove the front from the frame. Press the front face down on a towel to avoid flattening the stitches.

To finish

1 Cut out the front. Cut two 43 x 30cm rectangles for the back from fabric. Press under 2.5cm then 4cm on one long edge of the backs. Top stitch close to the outer pressed edge.

2 Make a vertical buttonhole 2cm in from the top-stitched edge on one back. Make another buttonhole 8cm above and below the centre buttonhole.

3 With right sides facing up, overlap the buttonholed edge over the other top-stitched edge by 4cm. Tack across the overlapped raw edges. Sew buttons under the button holes.

4 With the buttons undone and outer edges level, pin the backs to the front. Stitch the outer edges. Clip the corners, turn right side out and insert the cushion pad.

Words and make: Cheryl Owen. Photos: Barry Marsden

Partridge in a pear tree

Whether hung on a tree or adorning a gift, these jewel-bright embroidered decs are a gorgeous spin on a traditional theme

You will need

Finished size: one partridge 13 x 11cm & one pear 10.5 x 7cm

- Tracing paper and sharp HB pencil
- 30 x 15cm rectangle of bonding web
- 30cm square of turquoise, pink, yellow and lime-green felt
- Turquoise, pink, yellow and lime-green stranded cotton embroidery thread
- Air-erasable fabric pen
- Toy filling
- Matching sewing thread

Making paper patterns

Enlarge the partridge, comb, beak, pear, stalk and leaf patterns (on page 87) by 125% on a photocopier and trace off, adding the details. Cut out the patterns.

Cutting out

Cut one pair of partridge bodies, combs, beaks, outer pears, stalks and leaves from felt, referring to the photo for the colours. Turn the partridge and pear patterns over and trace the wing, tummy, eye and inner pear on to the paper backing of a piece of bonding web. Roughly cut out the pieces, leaving a margin around the edges.

Press the bonding web pieces to felt, referring to the photos for the colours. Cut out the pieces and peel off the backing papers. Press the tummy, wing and eye to the partridge and the inner pear to the outer pear.

Makes: Cheryl Owen. Styling and photos: Sussie Bell. Illustrations: Terry Evans

TOP TIP

We made these decs using straight stitch, chain stitch, stem stitch, fly stitch, and lazy-daisy stitch.

Embroidering the partridge

1 On one body, embroider stars on the tummy and the eye using straight stitch.

2 Embroider the broken lines on the tummy, wing and one comb using stem stitch.

3 Embroider along the dotted lines using chain stitch. Embroider a row of fly stitches between the dots on the wing, anchoring the stitches at the crosses.

Making the partridge

1 Pin the combs and beaks together with wrong sides facing. Then, use a single length of sewing thread to oversew the outer edges together.

2 Pin and tack the comb and beak under the embroidered partridge. Pin the partridges together with wrong sides facing. Use a single length of sewing thread to oversew the edges of the partridges together, catching in the comb and beak and leaving a 4cm gap. Stuff the partridge evenly, then oversew the gap closed.

Embroidering the pear

1 On one pear, embroider a line of stem stitch 3mm inside the edge of the inner pear and a line of chain stitch 3mm outside the edge of the inner pear.

2 Embroider the broken lines on the inner pear and one leaf with stem stitch. Embroider stars on the inner pear with straight stitches.

3 Embroider a lazy-daisy stitch between the end of the central lines and the dots on the inner pear.

Making the pear

1 Pin the stalks and leaves together with wrong sides facing. Then, use a single length of sewing thread to oversew the outer edges together.

2 Pin and tack the stalk under the embroidered pear. Pin the pears together with wrong sides facing. Use a single length of sewing thread to oversew the edges of the pears together, catching in the stalk and leaving a 4cm gap. Stuff the pear evenly then oversew the gap closed.

3 With right sides facing up, pin the leaf to the pear just below the stalk. Oversew the leaf to the pear.

Hanging the decorations

Thread two 25cm-long strands of embroidery thread on to a needle and insert through the decoration at the top of the stalk and top of the wing. Knot the ends together.

Note

To transfer the design to the decorations, pierce a hole at the end of the lines of the stars, at intervals along the broken and dotted lines, and at the dots and crosses. Place the pattern on the felt pieces and dot through the holes with an air-erasable pen before you start each area of embroidery. Refer to the photo for embroidery colours and embroider with three strands of embroidery thread.

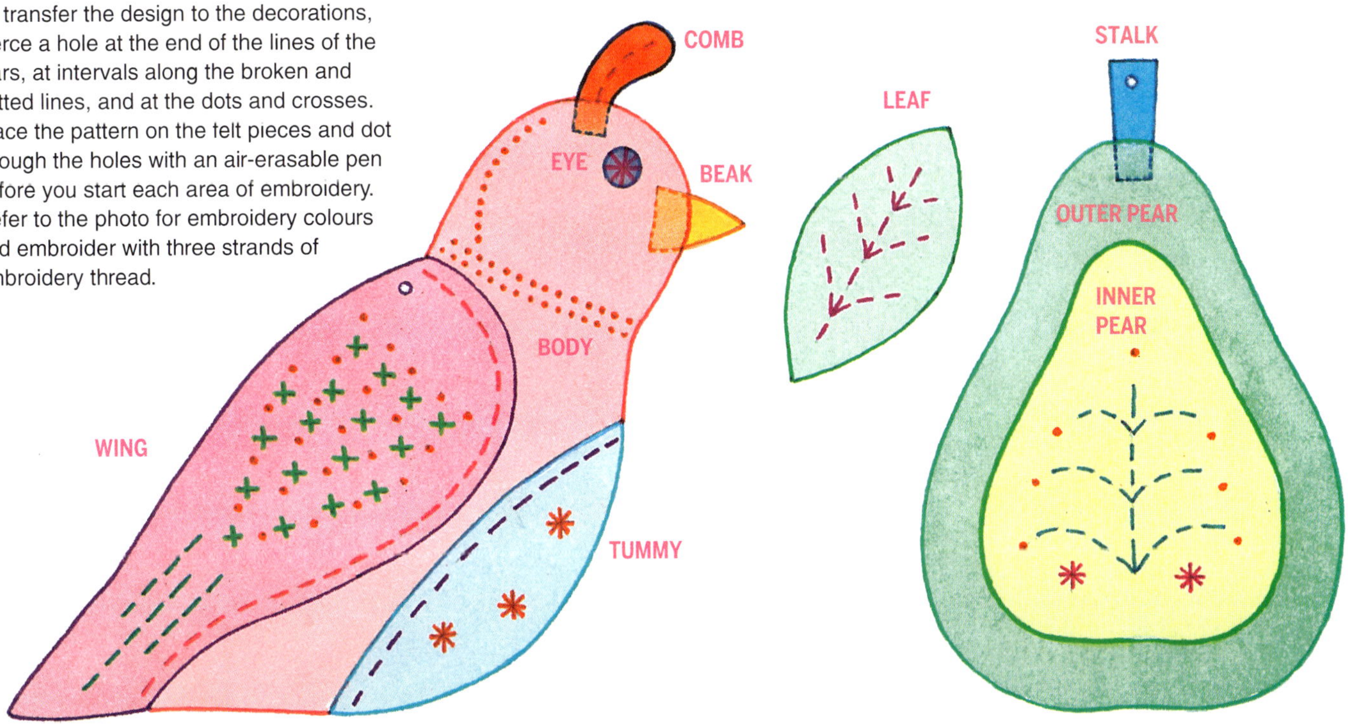

Enlarge templates by 125%

Forget-me-not cross stitch

These forget-me-nots are perfect for remembering those who have given their lives

You will need

Forget-me-not cross stitch
Finished size: 20 x 15cm

- 28 x 23cm rectangle of white 14 holes to 2.5cm Aida fabric
- Anchor stranded cotton embroidery thread in the following colours: 1 skein each of 97 (Mauve), 108 (Lilac), 136 (Blue), 255 (Green) and 290 (Yellow)
- Sharps size 8 sewing needle
- Size 24 tapestry embroidery needle
- 20 x 15cm picture frame with backing board
- Sewing thread for tacking
- Masking tape
- Strong sewing thread

Design chart

Key:

- 97 (Mauve)
- 255 (Green)
- 108 (Lilac)
- 290 (Yellow)
- 136 (Blue)

Sewing the design

Mark the centre of the Aida fabric lengthways and across the width with a line of tacking stitches worked through a row of holes, using a sewing needle.

Each coloured square on the chart represents one cross stitch worked over one block of fabric threads. The colour key above shows the colour of embroidery thread to be used. The centre of the design is marked with an arrow on each edge.

Using two strands of the six-stranded cotton and a tapestry needle, begin stitching near the centre of the fabric where the two lines cross. Work the stitches individually or in rows, following the chart and key. Work the lines with a back stitch, using two strands of the six-stranded cotton.

When complete, remove the tacking threads and press the work face down on a towel.

Framing the picture

Remove the backing board from the frame, then place the board on the centre of the wrong side of the embroidery. Pull the fabric firmly over two opposite edges and tape temporarily to the board with masking tape. Use a double length of strong thread and a needle to lace the taped edges, removing the tape as you sew. Repeat to lace the other two opposite edges together, tucking under the surplus fabric at the corners. Fix the embroidery in the frame.

Makes and words: Cheryl Owen. Photos: Barry Marsden, iStockphoto.com

Forget-Me-Not

TOP TIP

Try to use the selvedge of the denim for the strip at the bottom of the doorstop to look like the spray of the sea.

Set sail

Embrace this season's coastal trend and stitch this simple appliqué boat doorstop for your home

You will need

Boat doorstop

- 26 x 43cm sand fabric
- 10 x 53cm blue ticking fabric
- 20 x 43cm denim fabric
- White and navy sewing thread
- Scraps of fabric in red, white and blue Bondaweb
- Small resealable plastic bag
- Rice
- Stuffing
- 1m jute twine cord

Cutting out

From the denim fabric: cut out a 14cm diameter circle and a 5 x 43cm strip.

From the ticking fabric: cut out a 10 x 43cm strip, then a 6 x 10cm rectangle, for the applique boat. Fuse a piece of Bondaweb to the reverse of the appliqué boat following the manufacturer's instructions.

From the scrap fabrics: cut a white triangle sail measuring 4 x 6 x 7.2cm. Cut two blue and one red bunting triangles measuring 1.5cm on every side, and one red flag triangle measuring 2cm on every side. Fuse Bondaweb to all of the appliqué pieces.

Making the doorstop

1 Pin and sew the sand and ticking strips together along one long edge, with right sides facing and 1cm seam allowances. Press the seam towards the ticking fabric.

2 At the other long edge of the sand fabric, place the denim fabric over the top, so they overlap by 4cm. Pin together and topstitch the denim in place with wavy white lines of stitching.

3 Position the appliqué pieces in the centre of the sand section, using our image as a guide. Remove the paper backing and fuse in place with a warm iron. Top stitch the appliqués in place with a contrasting navy thread.

4 Fold the fabric in half with right sides facing so the two short edges meet. Pin and sew along the short edge with a 1cm seam allowance. Press the seams open.

5 Pin the denim circle to the bottom of the doorstop and stitch in place with right sides facing and 1cm seam allowance. Turn the doorstop right sides out and press.

6 Fold 6cm of the top ticking fabric over to the reverse so that wrong sides are facing and top stitch along the seam line to secure.

7 Fill the plastic bag with as much rice as you can spare — the more you use, the sturdier the doorstop will be. Seal the bag and position it in the bottom of the doorstop. Fill the rest of the doorstop with stuffing until it is plump and reaches the ticking band at the top.

8 Seal the doorstop by wrapping the twine around the top a couple of times and then tie in a bow at the front.

Words: Esme Clemo. Photos: Barry Marsden

Preparing the design

Enlarge a design (above) to your desired size, then trace off using a sharp HB pencil. Turn the tracing over and redraw the solid lines and dots. Mark the broken lines with a row of dots 5mm apart. Position the tracing right side up on the centre of the fabric and tape in place with masking tape. Redraw the design to transfer it to the fabric. Lay the fabric, with the lawn or voile underneath, if using it, right side up centrally on top of the inner ring of the hoop. Loosen the tension screw on the outer ring and press it over the inner ring, capturing the fabric. Make sure the fabric is smooth and the grain of the fabric straight. Tighten the screw to secure.

Hoops of fun

Follow these vibrant patterns to add some colour to your home

You will need

Embroidery hoops

- 25cm square of white even-weave fabric
- 25cm square of white cotton lawn or voile fabric (optional)
- 12.5cm-diameter embroidery hoop for arrows
- 15cm-diameter embroidery hoop for teacup, tree and number
- 17cm-diameter embroidery hoop for 'hello'
- 1 skein each of DMC stranded cotton embroidery thread in the following colours: 518 blue, 3806 pink, 741 orange, 958 green, 3706 peach
- Tracing paper
- Masking tape
- Sharp HB pencil
- Size 9 crewel needle
- Embroidery scissors

To start

Thread the needle with three strands of embroidery thread. To start stitching, leave a trailing end of about 2.5cm and catch it against the underside of the fabric while stitching. To finish, insert the needle through about 2cm of stitches on the back of the embroidery. Pull the thread through and cut off the excess.

1 For the teacup, using blue thread, bring the needle to the right side on the solid outline. Make a backward stitch 3mm long, bring the needle forward under the fabric to emerge 3mm ahead, ready to make the next stitch. Continue along the solid outlines.

2 Using pink thread, bring the needle to the right side at one end of one dotted line, insert the needle back through the same hole and bring it out at the next dot but do not pull the thread all the way through. Keeping the thread to the left of the needle, pull the needle through, forming loop of the chain. Continue to make stitches between the dots.

3 Using green thread, fill in the circle with straight stitches, make the stitches close to each other so that the background is covered and the outline is even and neat.

4 Using orange thread, bring the needle to the right side at the top of the circle, insert the needle back through the same hole and bring it out 5mm away with the thread under the needle. Pull the thread to make a loop. Insert the needle outside the loop to secure it. Make four lazy-daisy stitches at the quarter points around the circle then make a lazy-daisy stitch between the first ones. Using peach thread, make a lazy-daisy stitch between the dots either side of the central motif.

5 Using green thread, bring the needle out between the peach lazy-daisy stitches. Encircle the thread twice with the needle then turn the needle and insert it halfway through the fabric close to where it emerged, push the thread down the needle and pull it all the way through the fabric. Make a French knot between the other peach lazy-daisy stitches and at the dots along the base of the teacup.

6 Trim away the fabric 2cm from the outer ring of the hoop. Turn the hoop wrong side up and press the raw edges toward the back of the fabric. If you don't want to keep the embroidery in the hoop, remove it and press it face down on a towel.

Words and make: Esme Clemo. Photos: Barry Marsden

Fresh as a daisy

Pretty up crisp white linen and towels with our cross stitch flower project

You will need

Daisy embroidery

- 1 skein each of the following Anchor Stranded Cottons: 111 (Purple), 288 (Yellow) and 261 (Green)
- No.5 crewel needle
- No.20 tapestry needle
- 15.5cm embroidery hoop
- Rico Aida Band (2 pieces 4 x 110cm)
- DMC Soluble Canvas, 14 count
- Matching sewing threads

For perfect results

Don't knot your thread to start, as it will look unsightly in the finished piece. Anchor the thread by bringing the needle up through the back of the fabric and leave an end long enough to be caught in the next few stitches. Trim the end once secure. To finish, weave the end through the backs of five stitches and trim.

Working the stitch

A cross stitch is made over four holes in the canvas. Bring the needle up through the bottom left hole then, back down through the top right. Take the needle up through the bottom right hole and back down through the top left (see below). Repeat this stitch for blocks of colour.

To make rows of stitches in the same colour, bring the needle up at the bottom left hole and down through the top right. Continue this step for as many stitches as you need. Now work back along the row, bringing the needle up through the bottom-right hole and down through the top left.

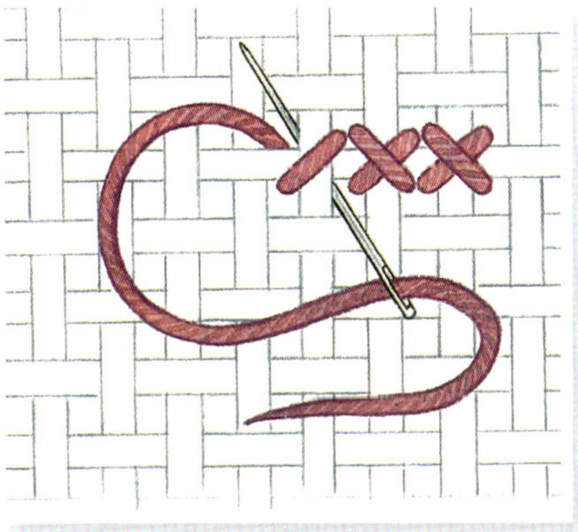

Stitching onto fabric

1 Cut a piece of soluble canvas slightly larger than the daisy motif; approx. 5cm for a single daisy, a 12cm square for the triple motif and 15 x 25cm for the larger motif used on the pillowcase.

2 Pin and tack the soluble canvas into position on the corner of your pillowcase or bag.

3 Using the chart on page 96 as your guide, work the daisy motifs using two strands of embroidery thread and the crewel needle.

4 To remove the soluble canvas, take off the tacking threads and dip the stitched area into a bowl of warm water (40-50°C) and leave for 5-10 minutes, while the canvas dissolves away. The stitched design will be left behind on the fabric.

5 Gently dot the embroidery with a towel to remove any excess water, and leave to dry. Press gently from the reverse side.

Working from a chart

Each coloured square on the chart represents one cross stitch. Follow the chart as you stitch, counting the number of stitches for each colour.

Daisy border

To add a pretty touch to the edge of a towel or laundry bag, work a daisy border along an Aida band and stitch in place.

1 Before you start, stretch the Aida band in the embroidery hoop. The fabric will have to be moved across inside the hoop as you complete each section.

2 Using two strands of embroidery thread, work a row of daisies. Move the fabric as needed.

3 Add a green border. Remove the band from the frame and lightly press on the reverse side. Pin and tack the embroidered band to the towel or bag, folding the raw edges under at both ends, and slip stitch in place around all edges.

TOP TIP

Use shorter pieces of thread, no longer than 30cm, to reduce the chances of creating knots and tangles.

Delightfully delicate

Embroider a graceful lily of the valley on to the corner of napkins and then paint the same design on to glassware for a floral display on your Easter table

You will need

Lily of the valley embroidery

- Tracing paper
- A sharp HB pencil
- Fawn linen or cotton napkin
- Mid-green, light green and white stranded cotton embroidery thread
- Crewel embroidery needle
- Matching sewing thread

Embroidering the napkin

Use two strands of embroidery thread and a crewel needle.

1 Trace the stem and leaves on to tracing paper and mark the tips of the flowers with a dot. Redraw the design on the wrong side of the tracing with a pencil.

2 Place the template right-side up on one corner of the napkin. Redraw the design to transfer it to the napkin.

3 Use stem stitch to embroider the leaf veins with mid-green embroidery thread and the stems with light green embroidery thread. Outline the leaves with back stitch, then fill in the leaves with long and short stitches using light green embroidery thread.

4 Embroider the flower petals using white embroidery thread with lazy-daisy stitches between the ends of the stems and the dots.

Template

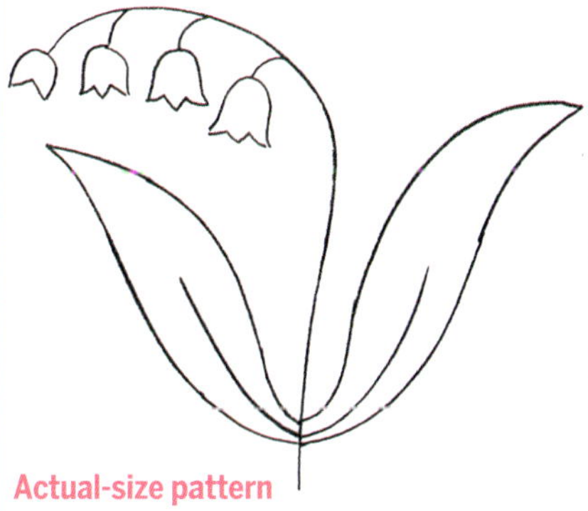

Actual-size pattern

112
134
114

104

Tricky Techniques

Push your limits with these intricate and more challenging projects

130

136

Hang on to cross stitch

Make your hall warm, welcoming and tidy with a giant cross stitch on a pegboard coat rack

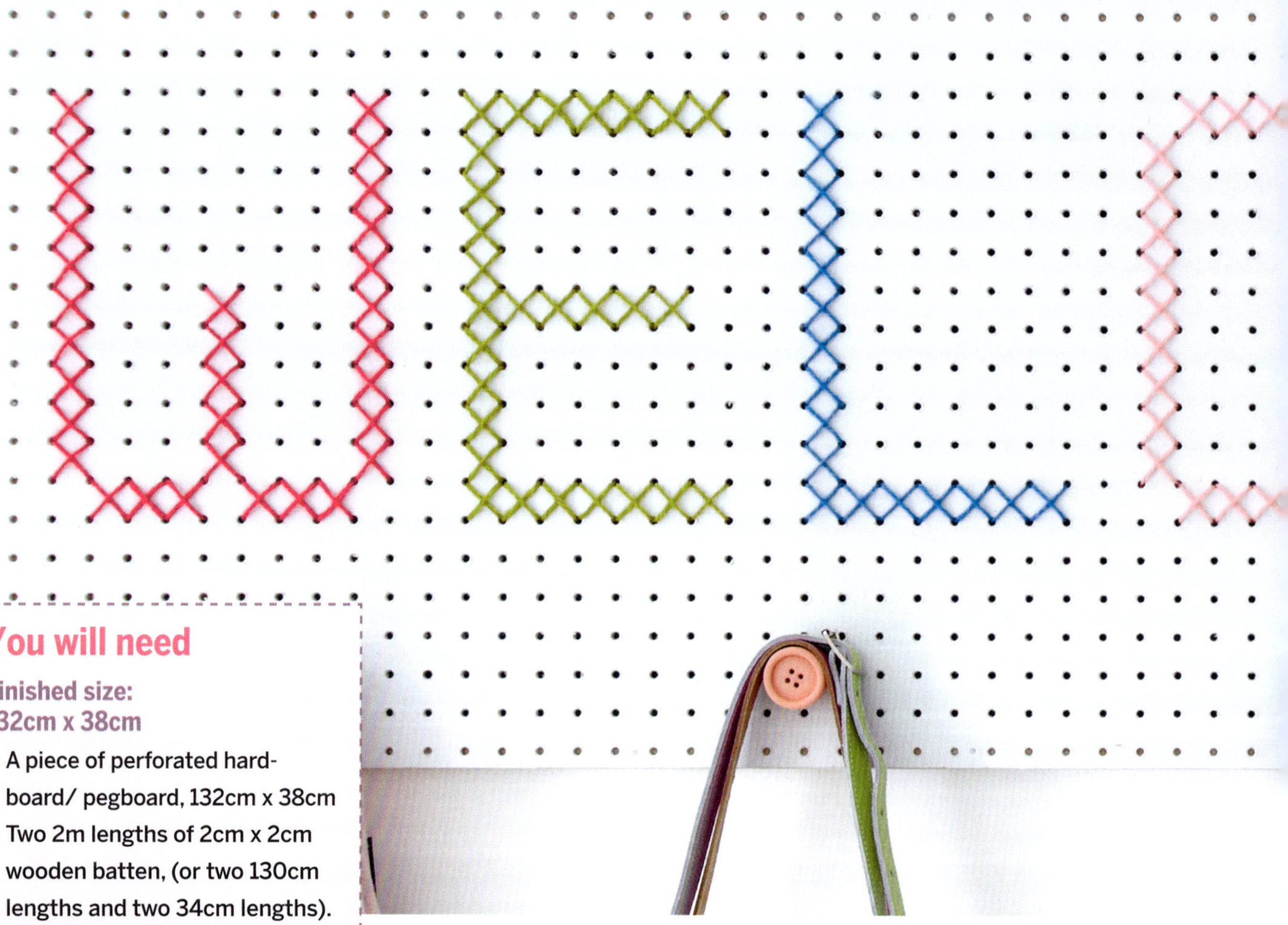

You will need

Finished size: 132cm x 38cm

- A piece of perforated hard-board/ pegboard, 132cm x 38cm
- Two 2m lengths of 2cm x 2cm wooden batten, (or two 130cm lengths and two 34cm lengths).
- Fine sandpaper
- Framing pins
- Tack hammer
- Spray primer and paint – we used Plasti-kote
- Anchor tapestry wools in seven colours – we used 8454 (Bright pink), 9198 (Green), 8806 (Turquoise), 8432 (Pale pink), 8018 (Yellow), 8774 (Pale blue), 9788 (Grey) and 8002 (Cream)
- Large tapestry needle
- Five coat hooks or door knobs

Photography: Ginette Chapman. Styling: Dilly Orme. Makes: Suzanne Clifen

1 Cut the pegboard to size, 132cm x 38cm or as required — your supplier might do this for you. Lightly sand the surface smooth.

2 You will need to attach a 2cm deep batten frame all around the back edges of the pegboard to keep it rigid and easy to hang. From two 2m battens, cut two 130cm lengths and two 34cm lengths. Then attach to the pegboard by knocking framing pins through the front, down into the batten frame behind.

3 Lightly spray an even coat of primer on to the pegboard and battens. Once dry, spray a coat of your chosen colour. Leave the pegboard to dry between coats, and apply more coats until you have an even base of colour. Leave overnight to ensure that the paint is completely dry.

4 Next, sew 'WELCOME' in cross stitch across the sprayed board, using the holes in the perforated board. Thread a large tapestry needle with tapestry wool and check that both the needle and wool fit through the holes with ease.

5 Start with your first letter by stitching into the third hole down from the top and second hole in from the edge. All the letters are 11 stitches down and most are seven stitches across depending on the width of

the letter. Each letter has one row of holes in between. Use the photo as reference for counting the stitches for each letter.

6 To start and finish each letter, leave long ends of wool on the back of pegboard and tie together to secure. The letters use a surprising amount of wool, so you will need to thread up more than once when stitching each letter, again tying ends together on the back.

7 Once your stitching is complete, attach and evenly space the button knobs along the bottom. You may need to cut these down a bit with a small hack saw so they sit flush with the wall.

Other ideas

Get all your stationery organised in one place — no more searching for the scissors!

Stitch your family name instead to create something truly unique.

Purple reign

Give classic white towels a French twist with this pretty lavender sprig design, worked in simple cross-stitch with couched 'bathroom' lettering

You will need

Tea towel

- Chart on this page
- A white waffle or terry towel with a 8cm wide flat border
- 12cm-wide strip of 14-count soluble waste canvas
- Anchor stranded cottons in the following shades: 876 (Green), 119 (Dark purple), 118 (Light purple) and 1 (White)
- Two no 24-26 tapestry needles
- Embroidery hoop
- Sewing thread
- Dressmaker's carbon paper

To stitch

1 Tack the piece of soluble canvas centrally to the towel's border, making sure that it is straight. Mark the centre of the waste canvas lengthways and widthways with a line of tacking stitches worked through a row of holes. Then, fix the fabric into the hoop.

2 The design is worked mainly in cross-stitch with couching stitch used for the lettering. If you are a beginner, practise the stitches on some spare waste canvas first.

3 The chart below shows the complete design. Each coloured square or symbol represents one cross-stitch worked over one square of fabric. The straight lines represent the couching.

4 Starting at the centre of the design and using two strands of embroidery thread in your needle, work all the main cross stitch areas, following the chart.

5 You can either leave your design with just the flowers or add the words 'Salle de bain' (bathroom). To do this, remove the work from the hoop and trace the lettering from the chart carefully using dressmaker's carbon paper. Fix your work back into the hoop and thread one needle with six strands of light purple (118) and a second needle with two strands of white (1). Bring both needles through from the back of the fabric and work the lettering by laying the purple thread along the design lines and couching it in place with the white.

6 Remove the work from the hoop and unpick the tacking. Put the embroidered fabric in hot, soapy water and soak until the waste canvas has dissolved away. Leave to dry and then press lightly on the wrong side under a damp cloth, taking care not to flatten the stitches.

Cross stitch chart

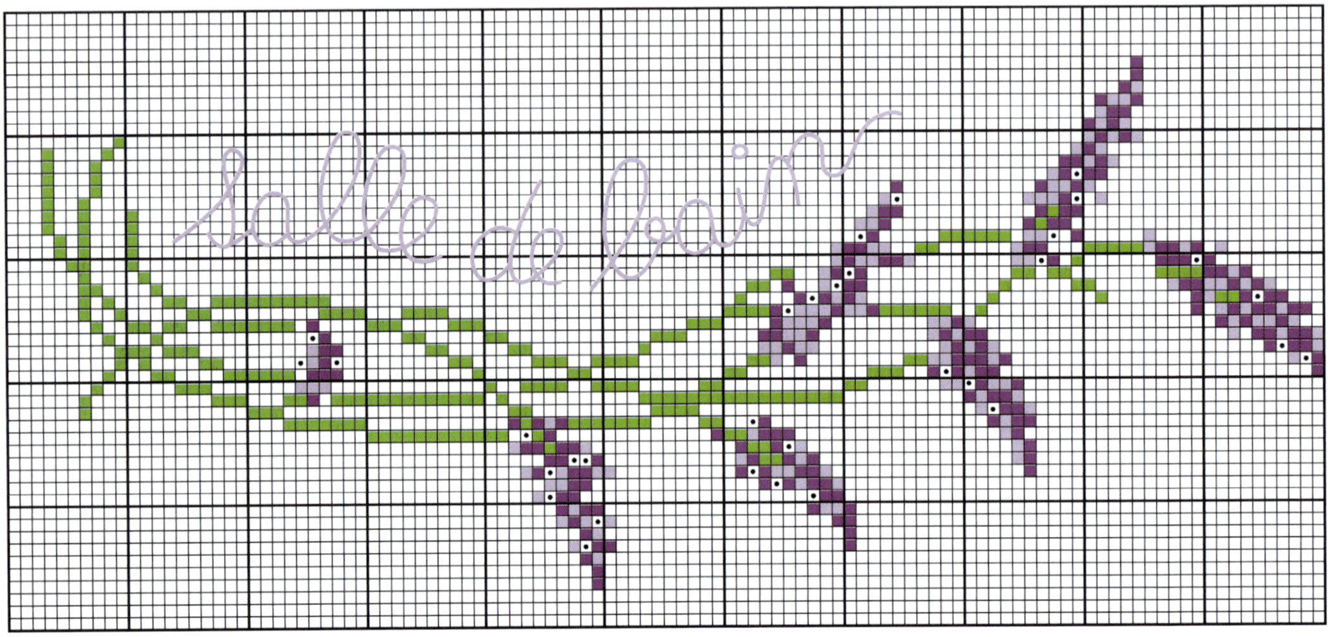

Key:

876 (Green) 119 (Dark purple) 118 (Light purple) 1 (White)

salle de bain

Fresh fruit

Embroider this colourful peach motif on to tea towels and create stylish cushions for your home

You will need

Finished cushion size: 38cm square

- Embroidery motif on page 105
- Smooth checked or plain tea towel
- Tracing paper and pencils, or dressmaker's carbon paper
- One skein each of Anchor stranded cotton in the following shades: 295 (Lemon yellow), 298 (Mustard yellow), 290 (Bright yellow), 303 (Orange), 359 (Dark brown), 228 (Bottle green), 227 (Medium green), 225 (Light green), 355 (Light brown), 13 (Red), 10 (Pink) and 302 (Peach)
- Crewel needle (size 6 or to suit fabric)
- Small embroidery frame
- Sharp embroidery scissors
- Matching sewing thread for making up cushion
- One cushion pad, 38cm square

TOP TIP

After photocopying the design, you may find it useful to use coloured pencils to mark each area in the correct shade, so that you can identify the stitched areas more easily.

Peach embroidery motif

Key

Satin stitch

A – 295 (Lemon yellow)
B – 298 (Mustard yellow)
C – 290 (Bright yellow)
D – 303 (Orange)
E – 359 (Dark brown)
F – 228 (Bottle green)
G – 227 (Medium green)
H – 225 (Light green)
I – 355 (Light brown)
J – 13 (Red)
K – 10 (Pink)
L – 302 (Peach)

Back stitch

═ – 13 (Red)

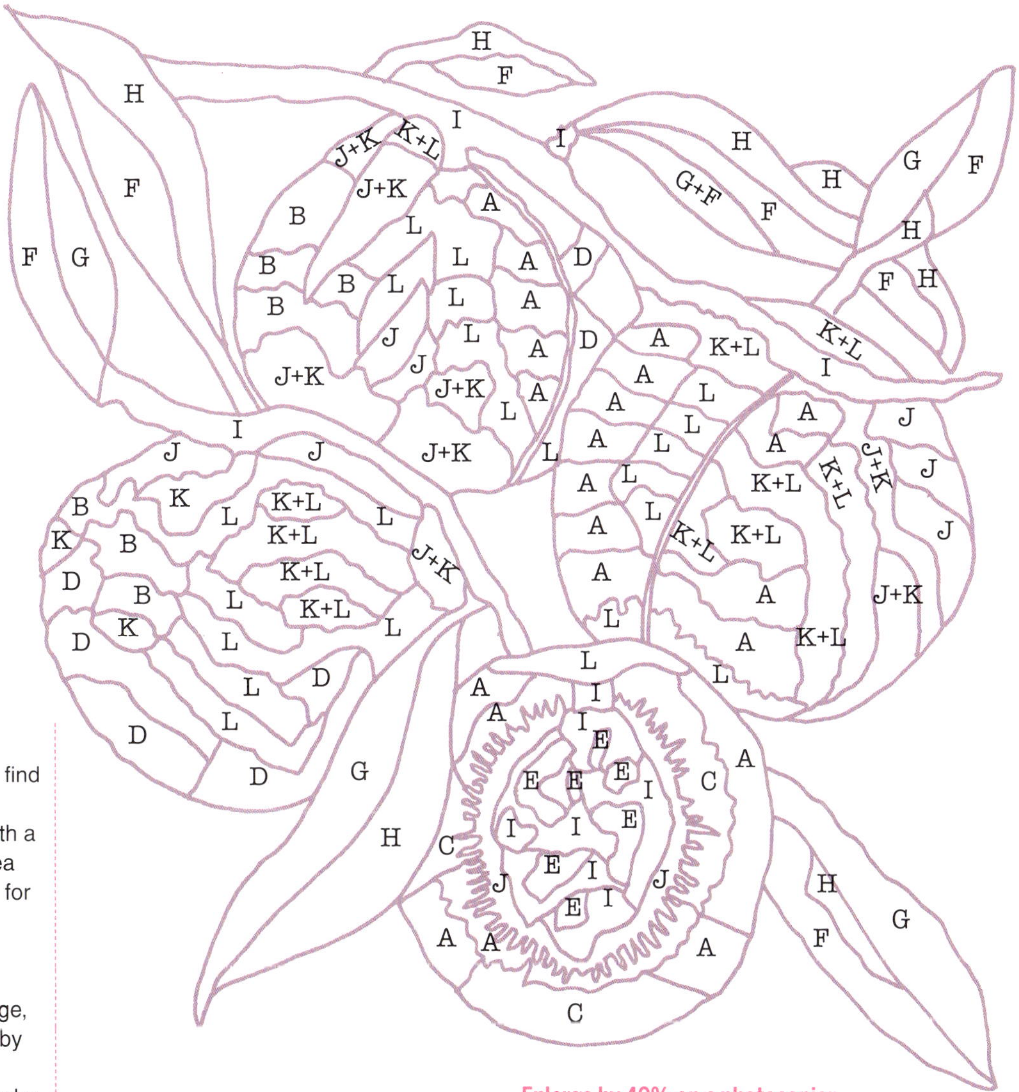

Enlarge by 40% on a photocopier

Preparing the tea towels

Cut a 41cm square from one tea towel, find the centre by folding the fabric in half vertically and horizontally, then mark with a pin or pencil dot. From the remaining tea towel, cut two oblongs, both 26 x 41cm for the cushion backs.

Tracing motifs

Photocopy or trace the motif on this page, enlarging by 40% and mark the centre by folding in half both vertically and horizontally. Matching up the central marks, transfer the motif to the fabric square using dressmaker's carbon paper, and following the manufacturer's instructions.

To embroider

1 Place the fabric square in the embroidery frame, making sure it's well stretched.

2 This design is worked in blocks of satin stitch using four strands of embroidery thread throughout. Work the branches and leaves first and then the fruit, following the colour key next to the chart and the photographs as a guide. In the areas marked with two colours, use two strands of each colour in your needle to give a variegated effect. Finally, work a row of back stitches as indicated.

3 Knots make the stitched surface lumpy, so always start a length of embroidery cotton by leaving a 2cm loose end on the wrong side of the fabric and stitch over it as you embroider. Run the end of a finished length of embroidery cotton through stitches on the wrong side of the work.

4 When you've finished the embroidery, place it face down on a padded ironing board, cover with a damp cloth and press lightly.

Making up the cushion

1 Neaten and hem one long edge of each oblong with a 1cm double-turned hem. Place one of these oblongs on to the embroidered square, with right sides together, raw edges matching and hemmed edge partly covering the stitched design then machine stitch together around the raw edges taking a 1.5cm seam allowance.

2 Place the second oblong at the opposite end of the embroidered square, with right sides together, raw edges matching and hemmed edge overlapping previous piece. Machine together around the three raw edges again taking a 1.5cm seam allowance. Turn right side out, press the seamed edges and insert the cushion pad.

Sashiko stitching

The geometric designs on these coasters are inspired by ancient Japanese techniques

Feature: Esme Clemo. Photos: Barry Marsden

You will need

Finished size: 10cm sq

- White sashiko embroidery thread
- 60cm square blue cotton fabric
- Sashiko embroidery needle
- Water-soluble fabric pencil
  30cm square low-loft batting
- Quilter's ruler
- Compass
- Scissors
- Sewing machine
- Matching sewing thread

Cutting out

To create four 10cm square coasters, cut eight 15cm squares from the blue cotton and four 13cm squares from the batting.

Making the pattern

1 Start by marking vertical lines at 2.5cm apart on four of the blue cotton squares using the quilting ruler and water-soluble pencil. Then, in the same way, mark horizontal lines at 2.5cm apart to create a square grid.

2 Find a cup or cookie cutter to draw around or use a compass to create circles inside groups of four squares. Repeat, overlapping the circles and using our photo as a guide. This pattern is traditionally called shippou.

3 If you don't want to worry about making your own pattern and washing away the grid lines afterwards, buy a stencil of the shippou pattern. Simply position the stencil on the cotton square and mark the pattern out with the water-soluble pencil.

4 The stitching technique is different from traditional European methods. Cut a piece of sashiko thread that's long enough to be worked from one side of the pattern to the other, and knot the end. Thread onto the sashiko embroidery needle and, starting on the wrong side of fabric, work the needle along the stitch line so that the fabric pleats along the needle. The stitches are similar to a running stitch, about 3mm long on the right side and 2mm on the reverse. Once you've completed a small section of the design or come to an intersection, pull the needle through the fabric to reveal the stitches left behind. Pull the fabric taut to eradicate puckering.

5 Work stitches in straight paths — so for this design you would stitch along the wavy lines rather than stitching a complete circle. Also for this pattern, ignore the original grid guidelines as they're not part of the stitched design.

6 On the reverse of the work, to help avoid puckering, leave long floats of thread between the intersections and turns in direction. Once stitched, tie off the loose threads and press flat.

7 Using the ruler and rotary cutter, trim the squares to 13cm. Pair a stitched blue square with a plain one, right sides together. Top with a square of batting and pin the layers together. Sew all around the edge with a 1.5cm seam allowance, leaving a small gap for turning through.

8 Clip the corners, turn right sides out and press. Turn the open edge inside the coaster and pin together. Slip stitch the gap closed with a matching thread. In the main image on the opposite page, we've created a sakura, seigaiha and fondou design, too, using Sew Easy sashiko templates.

You will need

Finished size: 40 x 30cm

- 50 x 50cm square of white 32 count linen fabric
- 2 skeins of Anchor 0149 (Navy) stranded cotton embroidery thread
- 1 skein of Anchor 0849 (Grey) stranded cotton embroidery thread
- 40cm of 110cm wide grey cotton fabric
- Four white 10cm tassels
- 40 x 30cm rectangular cushion pad
- Sharp HB pencil
- Contrast sewing thread for tacking
- 43 x 43cm embroidery frame (stretcher)
- Size 28 tapestry needle
- Matching sewing thread
- Zipper foot (optional)

Aztec cushion

This two-tone pattern will look pretty in any colours you choose

Aztec template

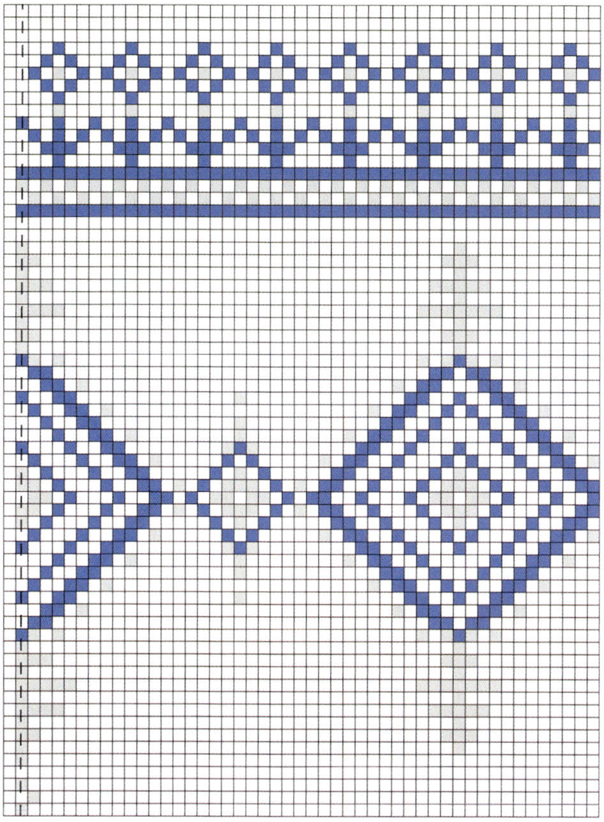

How to cross stitch

Each cross-stitch is taken over four threads of the fabric using three strands of embroidery thread in the needle. Each square on the chart represents 4 x 4 threads of the fabric. Bring the needle to the right side at the upper-left corner and insert it four threads down and four threads to the right, forming a diagonal stitch. Bring the needle to the right side four threads up. To complete an individual stitch, insert the needle four threads down and four threads to the left, making a diagonal stitch. Alternatively, continue to make a row of half-stitches then work back, completing the upper half of the crosses.

Embroidering the cross stitch front

1 Lightly draw a 43 x 33cm rectangle centrally on the linen with a pencil. Using contrast thread, sew a large running stitch vertically along the centre of the drawn rectangle, parallel with the long edges. Fix the linen centrally in the embroidery frame. Mark across the tacked line with a pin 6cm down from the upper drawn line.

2 Refer to the chart to embroider the design, removing the tacking stitches as you go. The broken line on the chart marks the tacked line. The pin marks the top row of the design. When you have completed the stitches on the chart, repeat to continue a mirror image across the fabric.

3 Remove the embroidery from the frame. Press the work face down on a towel. Cut out the rectangle along the drawn lines.

Making the cushion

1 Stitch seams with right sides facing and raw edges level, taking a 1.5cm seam allowance.

2 Cut two 33 x 29cm rectangles for the back from grey cotton. Press under 1cm then 1.5cm on one long edge of the backs. Stitch close to the inner pressed edges to hem the pieces.

3 With the outer edges level, pin the backs to the cushion front, overlapping the hemmed edges.

4 Stitch the outer edge, leaving a 3mm gap at the corners for the tassels. Slip one tassel into the cushion and pull its hanging loop through one corner gap. Using a zipper foot (if you have one) on the sewing machine, stitch across the loop a few times close to the corner. Repeat at each corner.

5 Clip the seam allowance at the corners, turn right side out and insert the cushion pad.

Perfect purse

Delicately embroidered and beaded, this stylish blue evening bag can be made in any colour to match a special outfit

You will need

Finished size: 19 x 17cm

- Access to a photocopier to enlarge pattern
- Tracing paper and sharp HB pencil
- 65 x 40cm rectangle of silk or polyester fabric
- 45 x 25cm rectangle of lightweight wadding and lining
- White stranded cotton embroidery thread
- Approx 26 x 3mm white pearl beads
- 30cm embroidery hoop
- Matching sewing thread
- Curved 13.5 x 9cm metal glue-in purse frame with loops
- Purse chain
- Masking tape
- Strong textile glue, eg, Gütermann HT2

Purse template

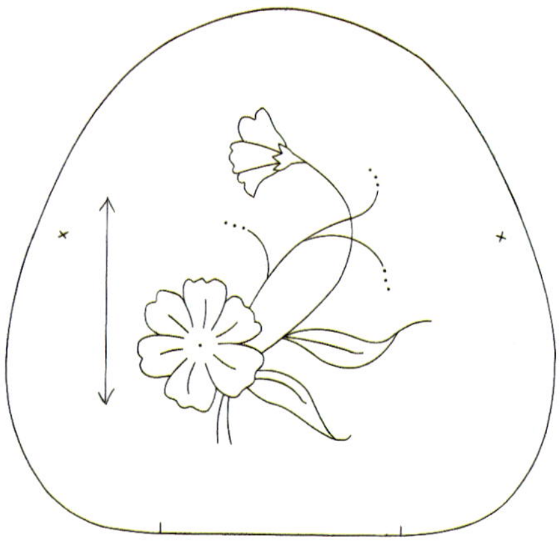

Enlarge by 360% on a photocopier

Making paper patterns

On a photocopier, enlarge the pattern to 360%. Trace the pattern onto tracing paper. Mark the crosses, notches, embroidery motif and dots with a pencil. Cut out the pattern. Redraw the embroidery motif and dots on the wrong side of the tracing with a pencil.

Cutting out

1 Ensure that arrows run in the same direction as the grain of the fabric.

2 Cut one 40 x 40cm square and one purse from fabric. Cut one pair of purses from wadding and lining.

3 Lightly draw the crosses and notches on the wrong side of the fabric and lining purses. Snip the notches. With right sides facing up, tape the pattern on the centre of the fabric square.

4 Draw around the pattern then redraw the embroidery motif and dots to transfer them to the fabric. Remove the pattern.

Making the purse

Note: Take a 1cm seam allowance and stitch seams with right sides together and raw edges level.

1 Cut out the embroidered purse, lightly draw the crosses and notches on the wrong side. Snip the notches. Tack the wadding to the wrong side of the fabric purses.

2 Pin and stitch the lower notched edges of the fabric purses together between the crosses. Clip the curves and press the seam open.

3 Repeat step 2 to make the lining, leaving a gap between the notches to turn through later. Turn the fabric purse right side out and insert it into the lining, matching the seams.

Embroidering the purse

Fix the fabric square right-side up centrally in the embroidery hoop. Pull the fabric taut. Use three strands of embroidery thread to embroider the motif with stem stitch. Sew a bead at the dots. Sew beads around the bead at the flower centre. Remove the embroidery. Press it face down on a towel, to avoid squashing the stitches.

4 Pin the upper edge of one purse and lining together. Starting at one cross, hand sew the upper edge with a neat back stitch for about 2cm. Repeat at the other end of the upper edge. Machine-stitch the upper edge between the hand-stitching. Repeat on the other upper edge. Carefully trim away the wadding in the seam allowances. Snip the curves.

5 Pull the purse right side out through the gap in the lining. Slip stitch the gap closed. Push the lining into the purse. Press the upper edges.

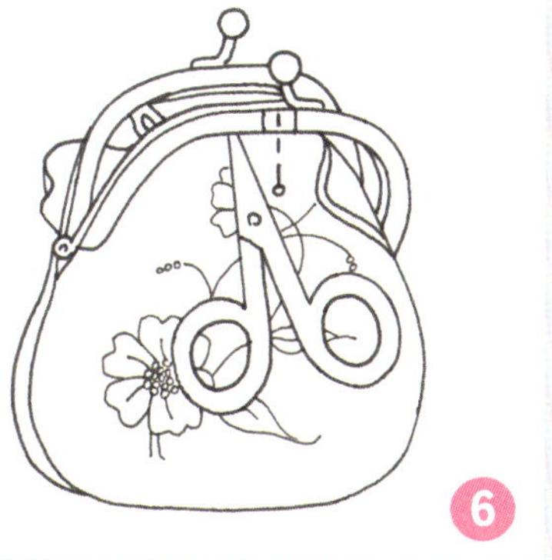

6 Stick a piece of masking tape to each section of the purse frame at the centre. Mark the centre on the tape with the pencil. Mark the centre of the upper edges of the purse with a pin. Open the frame wide. Follow the glue manufacturer's instructions to run a line of glue generously inside one channel of the frame. Apply glue to the upper edge of the purse front, starting and finishing 1.5cm above the intersection of the seams. (Leave to start to dry if instructed to do so.)

7 Insert the upper edge of the purse front into the frame channel, matching centres. Carefully ease the purse into the channel as far as it will go, using the tip of a scissor blade on the outside and then the inside of the purse. Leave to dry, then repeat on the upper edge of the purse back. Leave the glue to dry completely before handling. Clip the chain ends onto the loops.

TOP TIP

Don't worry if you get glue on the outside of the metal frame, it's easy to scrape off.

Make: Cheryl Owen. Photos: Barry Marsden

Go wild

Jump on the wildlife trend by stitching your own bear tote bag

You will need

Bear tote bag

- Tracing paper
- Transfer pencil
- Black embroidery thread
- 46cm of 152cm-wide heavy cotton fabric in yellow
- 30cm x 30cm heavy cotton fabric in white
- 30 x 30cm lightweight iron-on interfacing
- Black sewing thread
- Scissors
- Sewing machine

TOP TIP

Don't fancy a bear? Sketch your own animal design straight onto the fabric, ready to be stitched.

Bear template

Feature: Esme Clemo. Photo: Barry Marsden/ti-mediacontent.com

Enlarge by 230% on a photocopier

Cutting out

For the bag: Cut out two 38 x 45cm rectangles from the yellow fabric.

For the handles: Cut out two 8 x 60cm strips from the yellow fabric.

Making the bag

1 Fuse the iron-on interfacing to the reverse of the white cotton, making sure to follow the manufacturer's instructions for dampening the fabric with a wet cloth and the heat setting to use.

2 Enlarge the template by 230%. Using the transfer pencil and a piece of tracing paper, trace the embroidery design from the template. Place the tracing paper on the white fabric with tracing side down. With an iron set on low, press the paper to the fabric to transfer the design. Gently peel away the paper to reveal the bear design beneath.

3 With black thread and a small zigzag stitch, carefully sew over all the markings on the fabric. Use a larger zigzag stitch to fill in the nose and eye sections. For the wobbly lines, go over the areas twice to give the design a 'sketched' look. Once complete, press the appliqué and cut away the excess fabric close to the outline edge.

4 Position the appliqué on the lower right corner on the front of one of the bag pieces. Pin and sew all the way around the edge with a straight stitch. Try to stitch on top of the zigzag stitches to conceal the straight stitches.

5 Turn the top edge of both bag pieces under by 2cm and then another 2cm. Pin and stitch as close to the folded edge as possible with black thread to secure.

6 For the handles, press the strips in half lengthways. Open out the strip and

turn the raw edges under by 1cm along the long edges. Re-fold along the original crease to conceal the raw edges and pin. Top stitch along the turned edge with black thread. Turn up the short ends by 2cm and press.

7 Position the handles on the wrong side of the bag pieces, about 3cm from the top of each bag piece and 11cm in from either side. Make sure that the turned up ends are facing the bag. Pin and sew in place with a stitched square, reinforced with a cross.

8 Pin and sew the bag pieces together with right sides facing and 1cm seam allowances. Stitch around the side and bottom edges. Clip the corners, turn right sides out and press.

ABCDE
FGHIJK
LMNOP
QRSTU
VWXYZ

Lovely letters

Our pretty, eye-catching A-Z sampler uses a variety of embroidery stitches in bright vivid colours. Stitch the whole design or focus on one or two individual letters

You will need

Sampler

- Access to a photocopier
- 40 x 30cm rectangle of grey evenweave fabric
- 30cm-diameter embroidery hoop
- 1 skein each of Anchor stranded cotton embroidery thread in the following colours: 1 (White), 25 (Pale pink), 27 (Mid pink), 28 (Deep pink), 086 (Mauve), 0187 (Turquoise), 0239 (Green), 0297 (Yellow), 0313 (Apricot) and 0314 orange
- Tracing paper
- Masking tape
- Sharp HB pencil
- Two size 9 crewel needles
- Embroidery scissors
- A4 piece of white card
- Strong sewing thread

TOP TIP To keep back stitch and chain stitches evenly sized, mark equal stitch lengths against the letter with an air-erasable fabric pen.

Preparing the design

Enlarge the template (page 117) to 150% on a photocopier. Trace off the solid and broken lines and dots on to the centre of the fabric, securing the tracing paper in place with masking tape. Lay the fabric right side up centrally on top of the inner ring of the hoop. Loosen the tension screw on the outer ring and press it over the inner ring, capturing the fabric. Ensure the fabric is smooth and the grain is straight. Tighten screw to secure.

Embroidering the alphabet

Use three strands of embroidery thread in a crewel needle throughout, unless stated otherwise. To start stitching, leave a trailing end of thread about 2.5cm long and catch it against the underside of the fabric while stitching. To finish, insert the needle through about 2cm of stitches on the back of the embroidery. Pull the thread through and cut off the excess.

A Use six strands of orange thread for the couching stitch. Oversew in place with mauve thread.

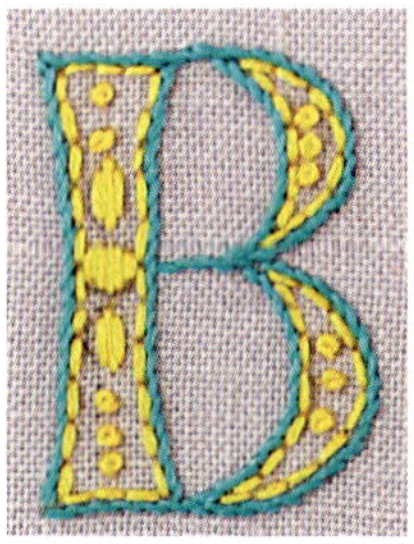

B Stitch the outline with stem stitch using turquoise thread. Then, use yellow thread to stitch the shapes with satin stitch, make French knots at the dots, and stitch just inside the outline with back stitch.

C Stitch the outline with looped back stitch using mid-pink thread for the back stitch and orange thread for the loops.

D Use lazy-daisy stitches radiating out from the circle to the outer dots with white thread. Use yellow thread to stitch along the broken line with chain stitch, with a lazy daisy-stitch to the dots at each end of the line, then fill the circle with yellow French knots.

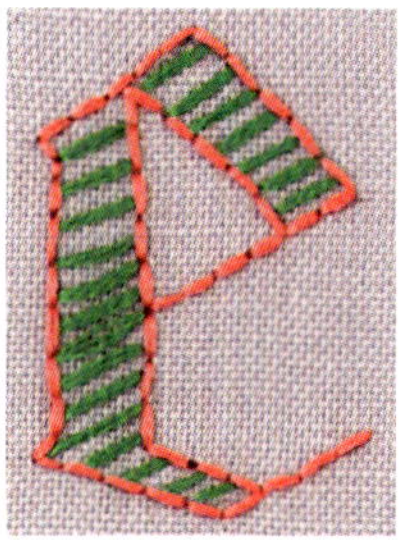

E Fill the diagonal straight stitches 3mm apart using green thread. Stitch the outline with back stitch using mid-pink thread.

F Use turquoise thread to blanket stitch the letter, making the stitches close together and 5mm deep.

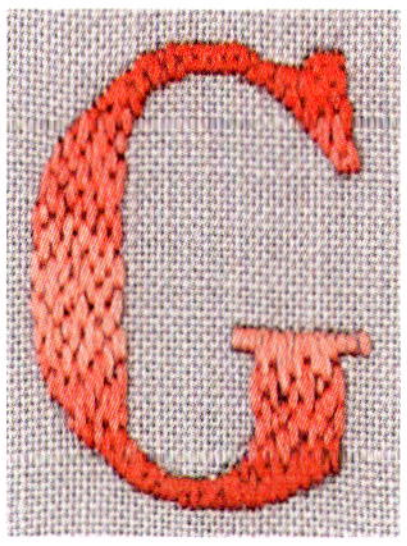

G Fill the letter with long and short stitch using the horizontal lines as a guide to change colour. Start with deep pink at the top and bottom, then mid pink, then pale pink in the centre.

H Stitch along the broken lines with chain stitch using green thread, then stem stitch along the solid lines with white thread.

I Fill the circle with satin stitch and stitch the broken line with threaded running stitch, using mid pink thread for the running stitch and yellow for threading. Stitch straight stitches radiating out from the circle to the dots with yellow thread.

J Stitch the outline with stem stitch using turquoise thread. Stitch chain stitch along the dots with orange thread.

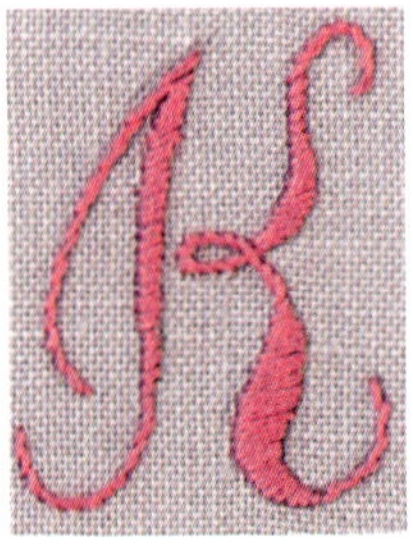

K Using mauve thread, stitch the letter with satin stitch for the shapes and stem stitch for the lines.

L Stitch along the broken lines with chain stitch, then stitch again just inside the outline using mauve thread.

M Use orange thread to stitch the uprights of the letter with fly stitches between the dots, making the anchoring stitches at the straight lines, then stitch the diagonal lines with fly stitches.

N Make a star stitch at the dots, making the straight stitches of the top star 4mm long and the bottom stars 3mm long, using white thread. Stitch along the broken lines with chain stitch, making a lazy daisy at the top of the letter and then make three lazy daisy stitches facing inwards from the left-hand upright line, using turquoise thread. Use turquoise thread to make a French knot at the centre of the stars.

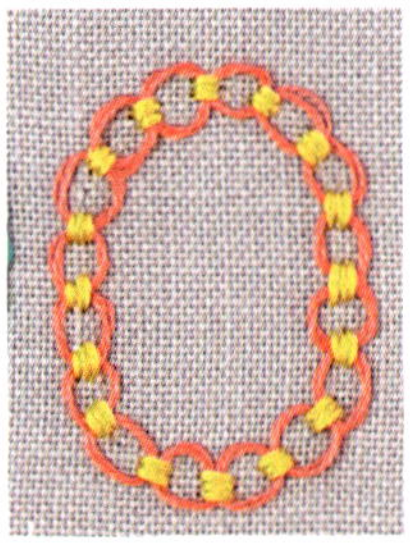

O Stitch the letter with guilloche stitch, using yellow thread for the straight stitches and mid pink thread for the threading stitch.

P Stitch the leaves with satin stitch using green thread. Make a French knot at the dots using white thread. Fill in the inner sections of the letter with French knots using apricot thread then fill in the outer sections with French knots using orange thread.

TOP TIP

If framing your picture in an A4 frame, lace the embroidery over the frame's backing board instead of using a separate piece of card.

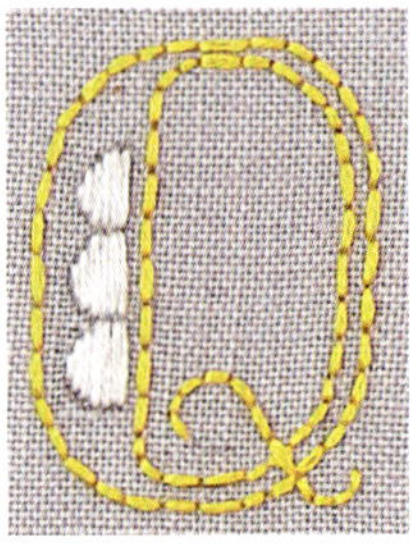

Q Use yellow thread to stitch the outline with back stitch. Stitch the scallops in satin stitch using white thread.

R Refer to the picture to stitch the letter with straight stitches and satin stitch for the solid shapes, using a mixture of green and turquoise thread. Stitch the broken lines with back stitch using green thread.

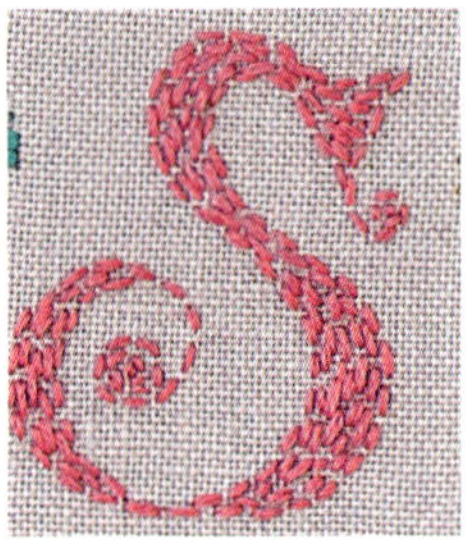

S Stitch the outline with small running stitches, then fill in the letter with small single straight stitches using mauve thread.

T Stitch with cross stitch between the dots using yellow thread.

U Stitch the lines with whipped stem stitch using white thread for the stem stitch and mid pink thread for the whipping.

V Use mauve thread to stitch the petals with satin stitch. Make a French knot at the centre of the flower using yellow thread. Stitch the outline of the letter in stem stitch using orange thread.

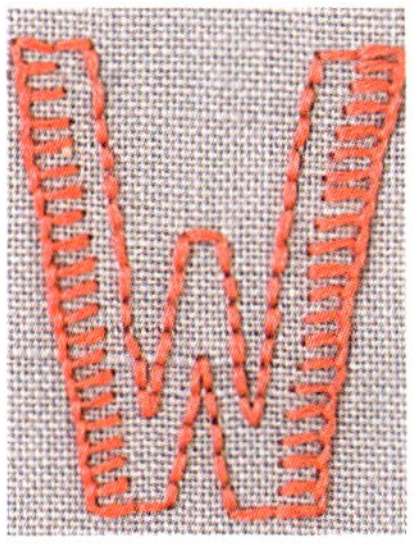

W Stitch the outer edge of the uprights with blanket stitch 4mm deep, then stitch the rest of the outline with back stitch using mid-pink thread.

X Stitch a star at each dot using yellow thread, making the straight stitches of the corner stars 4mm long and of the other stars 5mm long. Make a French knot at the centre of the stars with white thread.

Y Use green thread to stitch the letter with open fishbone stitch.

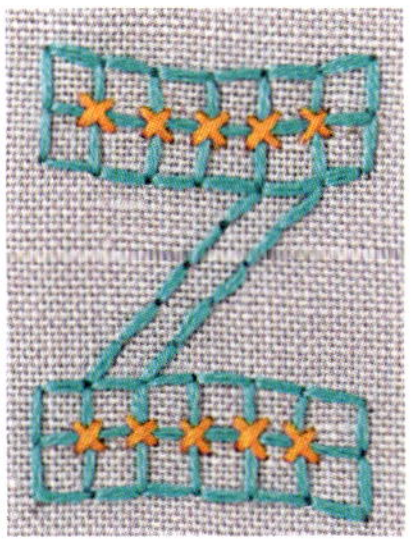

Z Stitch the diagonal lines of the letter with back stitch using turquoise thread. Embroider the horizontals of the letter with open filling stitch, using turquoise thread for the grid and orange thread for the cross stitches.

Alphabet template

Enlarge by 150% on a photocopier

To finish

Remove the embroidery from the hoop. Press the embroidery face down on a towel to avoid flattening the stitches. With the embroidery face down, position an A4 piece of card centrally on top. Thread a needle with a long double length of strong sewing thread. Fold the fabric over two opposite sides. Fasten the thread to the centre of one of these raw edges, then lace the thread back and forth between the raw edges, pulling the thread firmly. Fasten the thread ends securely then repeat, working in the other direction. Lace the other opposite edges in the same way, folding under the corners neatly.

You will need

Finished size: 40 x 40cm

- 43 x 43cm square of tracing paper
- Pencil
- 50cm of 110cm-wide green cotton or linen fabric
- 10 x 25cm rectangle of light green cotton fabric
- 30cm embroidery hoop
- 2 skeins of Anchor Perle 5 embroidery thread in dark pink 28 and light pink 25
- 1 skein of Anchor Perle 5 embroidery thread in light green 254, yellow 295 and white 1
- Air-erasable fabric marker
- 10 x 25cm rectangle bonding web
- Large crewel embroidery needle
- Matching sewing thread
- 40cm square cushion pad

Blooming lovely

Stitch up this embroidered floral cushion for your home

Making the paper pattern

On a photocopier, enlarge the pattern to 275%. Trace the motifs, dots and letters onto tracing paper. Redraw the motifs and dots on the wrong side of the tracing paper with a pencil; do not trace the broken lines of the flower bases, leaves and letters.

Preparing the cushion front

1 Trace the flower bases and leaves onto the paper backing of bonding web. Press the bonding web to the wrong side of light green cotton fabric. Cut out the pieces. Peel off the backing papers.

2 Draw a 43 x 43cm square on your chosen fabric for the cushion front. Pin the pattern right-side up on the fabric, matching the outline. Redraw the tracing to transfer the design onto the fabric.

3 Slip the flower bases and leaves under the tracing, matching positions. Lift the tracing and press the pieces in place. Remove the tracing.

Floral template

Enlarge by 275% on a photocopier

Embroidering the cushion front

Fix the cushion front in an embroidery hoop. Move the hoop when you have finished embroidering the motifs within it and move onto the next area to be embroidered.

Turkey stitch: Use two strands of embroidery thread using dark pink for rows A and B and light pink for rows C and D on the large flowers and yellow for rows A and B and light pink for rows C and D on the small flowers.

1 Don't knot the thread to start. Starting 2mm in from the left-hand end of row A, insert the needle to the wrong side, leaving a 2.5cm tail of thread. Bring the needle to the right side 4mm in from the left-hand end of the row. Back stitch to the start of the row.

2 Reinsert the needle to the right side where the tail thread or previous loop is and make a 4mm stitch, leaving a loop of thread measuring 2.5cm on the right.

3 Bring the needle to the right side 2mm along from the loop and make a back stitch to the end of the previous back stitch. Repeat steps 2 and 3 to complete the row.

4 Repeat on row B making the tail and loops 3cm long, on row C making the tail and loops 2.5cm long and row D making the tail and loops 3cm long. Snip through the loops to make a fringe. Trim the fringe of rows A and B level, then the fringe of rows C and D level 1cm below the upper rows.

Stem stitch

Use two strands of light green embroidery thread to create the flower stems and side of the bonding web flower bases. Use one strand of white thread to embroider the seed head stems.

Straight stitch

Refer to the pattern and use a strand of light green embroidery thread to embroider the leaf veins with straight stitches.

French knots

Use one strand of embroidery thread to embroider a French knot on the dots of the dotted outline of the large flower bases in yellow and the small flower bases in white. Fill these flower bases with French knots. Use one strand of white embroidery thread to embroider a French knot at the centre of seed heads.

Lazy-daisy stitch

Use one strand of white embroidery thread to embroider three lazy-daisy stitches at the end of the seed-head stems between the dots. Embroider lazy-daisy stitches between the dots along the stems, too. Use one strand of dark pink embroidery thread to embroider long lazy-daisy stitches along the stems of the small flowers between the dots.

Seed stitch

Use two strands of embroidery thread to embroider seed stitches on the bonding web flower bases of the large flowers in white and small flower bases in dark pink.

Sewing the cushion

1 Cut out the cushion front. Cut two 30 x 43cm rectangular pieces for the back from the fabric. Press under 1cm, then 1.5cm on one long edge of the backs. Stitch close to the inner press edges to hem the pieces.

2 With the outer edges level, pin the backs to the cushion front, overlapping the hemmed edges. Stitch the outer edge with 1.5cm seam allowances. Clip the corners, turn right side out and insert the cushion pad.

HO

Going country

Give classic cross stitch a fresh country feel with these five pretty projects using simple colours on slubby linens and crisp cotton fabrics

You will need

Motif size: approx 20.5 x 13.5cm

- Chart on page 129
- 50cm of 150cm-wide 10-count natural coloured Evenweave fabric
- Blue stranded embroidery thread
- No 24-26 tapestry needle
- Embroidery frame or hoop
- Matching sewing thread
- Enough flame-retardant polyester stuffing to fill the finished cushion cover

Cushion

1 Fold your fabric in half by bringing the two selvedges together (the finished edges down each side of the fabric) and cut into two equal pieces along the fold. Find the centre of one piece by folding and tacking. Fix one piece of fabric into the hoop or frame and, using three strands of embroidery thread, make the first cross-stitch at this central point. Follow the chart on page 129 to work the rest of the design on to the fabric.

2 Remove the fabric from the hoop and, keeping the stitched motif central and square, trim the fabric down to 30 x 45cm. Trim the second piece of fabric to match.

3 With right sides facing and raw edges level, stitch the two cover pieces together along the long sides, taking 1.5cm seam allowance. Turn to the right side and press the seams flat. Machine-stitch one short end together, 7cm out from the edge of the cross-stitch design, reverse stitching at each end to secure. Sew a second row, this time working 1cm out from the first line of stitching. Fill the cushion with polyester stuffing, pin, tack and then machine stitch twice at the other end of the cushion in the same way.

4 To create the fringes, fray the cushion fabric up to the stitching along both short edges by carefully pulling out the shorter cross threads.

You will need

Finished size: approx 4 x 3cm

- Chart on page 128
- Plain linen or cotton napkin
- 14-count soluble waste canvas
- Red stranded embroidery thread
- No 24-26 tapestry needle
- Embroidery hoop
- Sewing thread

Napkins

1 Tack a piece of soluble canvas about 5cm square in one corner of the napkin. Fix the fabric in a hoop and, following the chart on page 128, work the design with two strands of red embroidery thread.

2 Remove the work from the hoop and unpick the tacking. Dissolve the canvas away.

3 Leave to dry and then press lightly on the wrong side under a damp cloth taking care not to flatten the stitches.

You will need

Approx 7 x 5cm

- Chart on page 128
- 30cm of 112–150cm-wide 10-count linen evenweave fabric
- 14-count soluble waste canvas
- Red and blue stranded embroidery thread
- No 24-26 tapestry needle
- Embroidery hoop
- Matching sewing thread
- Double-sided sticky tape
- 25mm-wide iron-on hemming tape

Book cover

1 Open your notebook and press on the spine so it lies as flat as possible. Cut a rectangle of fabric that's one-and-a-half times the total width of the open book, plus 6cm, by the height of the book plus 6cm. Fold under a 2.5cm hem along each short end and secure the hems in place with the fusible hemming tape.

2 Wrap the fabric around the book and fold the excess fabric under the covers to form the inside facings. Place pins at the top and bottom of the spine and down each side of the spine to mark where the fabric fits and where it folds under the edges of the front and back covers. Remove the fabric from the book and tack along the four vertical pinned lines and across the top and bottom horizontal lines. Remove the pins.

3 Using the tacking lines and the photograph as a guide, fold the front section of the fabric into quarters to find the centre point for the cross stitch design. Fix the fabric in a hoop, with the tacked-cross placed centrally. Work the design in three strands each of red and blue embroidery thread according to the chart. If you like, you can add a border along the top and bottom, using the border on the cushion chart as a rough guide.

4 Remove the cover from the hoop and place, right side up, on a flat surface. With right sides facing and raw edges level, fold over the facing at each end of the cover and stitch along the top and bottom of each one, taking a 2.5cm seam allowance. Trim away the seam allowances at the corners and turn through to the right side. Press flat and press a 2.5cm hem along the remaining top and bottom edges of your fabric cover. Slip a strip of fusible hemming tape under each hem and iron to fix them in place. Fold the notebook's covers back and slip the cover in place.

You will need

Motif size: approx 20.5 x 13.5cm

- Chart on page 129
- Linen band, at least 75mm-wide
- 14-count soluble waste canvas
- Blue stranded embroidery thread
- No 24-26 tapestry needle
- Embroidery hoop
- Matching sewing thread
- Strong double-sided sticky tape

Shelf trim

1 Cut a length of linen band to fit the length of your shelf, plus 4cm. Press and stitch a double-turned 1cm hem to the wrong side along each short end. Cut a strip of soluble canvas to fit the width of your band and tack it in place. Following the chart on page 129, work the cross-stitch design, scaling it up to seven stitches per 2.5cm, i.e. work each stitch across two threads of your waste canvas, using three strands of embroidery thread in your needle.

2 Attach to the band, adding extra strips of soluble canvas as necessary, until you reach the end.

3 Remove the tacking and dissolve the waste canvas. Leave to dry and then press lightly on the wrong side under a damp cloth taking care not to flatten the stitches.

4 Fix in place along the shelf using double-sided tape.

You will need

Motif size: approx 10cm square

- Chart on page 128
- Pre-washed ready-made cotton pillowcase
- 14-count soluble waste canvas
- Red stranded embroidery thread
- No 24-26 tapestry needle
- Embroidery hoop
- Sewing thread

Pillowcase

1 Tack a piece of soluble canvas to one corner of the pillowcase. Fix the pillowcase in an embroidery hoop and, following the chart on page 128, work the cross-stitch design, scaling it up to seven stitches per 2.5cm, i.e. work each stitch across two threads of your waste canvas, using three strands of embroidery thread in your needle.

2 Remove and refit the pillowcase in the hoop to work a second motif on the adjacent corner of the pillowcase (or in all four corners if you prefer).

3 Once you have finished, remove the pillowcase from the hoop, remove the tacking stitches and dissolve the waste canvas. Leave to dry and then press lightly on the wrong side under a damp cloth taking care not to flatten the stitches.

Templates

Napkin

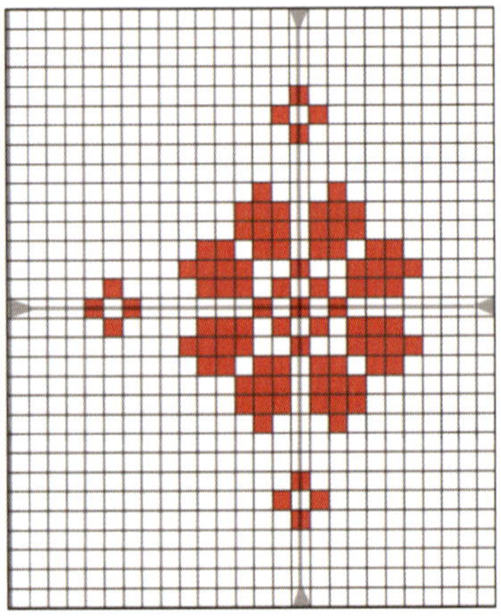

Pillowcase

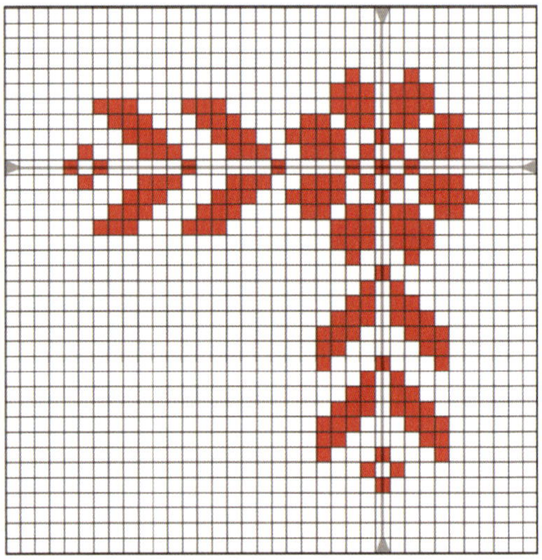

Book cover

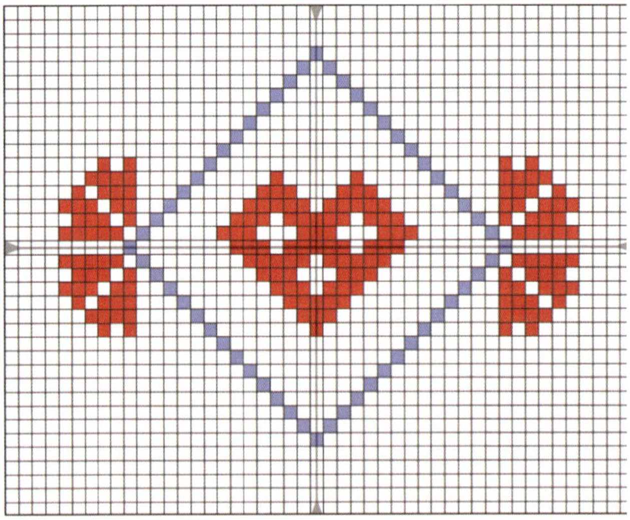

Shelf trim

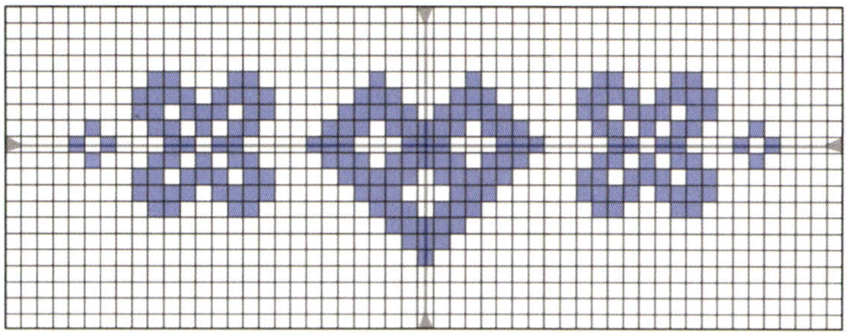

Cushion

Martha's
needlework box

Sew organised

Create a cute box to store your needlework equipment and works in progress

You will need

Finished size: 25 x 23cm, excluding loop

- Tracing paper
- A sharp HB pencil
- 40cm of 90cm-wide plain red felt
- 40cm of 112cm-wide turquoise patterned cotton fabric
- 40cm of 90cm-wide lightweight wadding
- 40cm of 90cm-wide turquoise felt
- 20cm of 90cm-wide white felt
- 30cm of 45cm-wide bonding web
- Three A3 sheets of 2-3mm thick card
- One 1cm white button
- Navy and red stranded cotton embroidery thread
- Matching sewing threads
- Fabric glue
- Access to a photocopier

TOP TIP You can use paper clips to hold the glued edges of the box in place while the glue dries.

Making the paper patterns

1 Using a photocopier, enlarge the pattern templates by 145%, then trace the patterns on to folded tracing paper, matching the broken lines to the fold.

2 Mark the outlines and grain line arrow. Cut out the patterns and open them out flat.

Cutting out

1 Ensure that the arrow runs in the same direction as the grain of the fabric, then cut straight edges parallel with the grain of the fabric.

2 Cut three houses (for the front, back and base), two 17cm squares for the side panels, and two 13 x 3.5cm rectangles for the loop from red felt. Cut three 24 x 16cm rectangles for the front, back and base linings and two 16cm squares for the side-panel linings from patterned fabric and wadding. Cut two 27 x 16cm rectangles for the roof and two gables from turquoise felt. Cut two 26 x 16cm rectangles for the roof linings and two gables from patterned fabric.

3 Trace two borders for the houses, two borders for the side panels, one door frame, two window frames, one door, two windows and six tulips on to the paper backing of bonding web, leaving a margin around each motif. Roughly cut out the pieces, leaving a margin all around.

4 Peel off the backing papers. Press the borders, door frame and window frames on to white felt. Press the door, windows and tulips on to turquoise felt. Cut out the pieces neatly. Peel off the backing papers.

5 Cut one 22 x 13.5cm rectangle for the base, two 22 x 14cm rectangles for the front and back, two 14 x 13cm rectangles for the side panels, two 24 x 13cm rectangles for the roof and two gables, cutting along the 'card cutting lines' from card.

Making the house

Note: Take 1.5cm seam allowance. Join pieces with right sides together and edges level.

1 Press the borders to the upper edge on the right side of the felt front, back and side panels, press the other pieces to the front. Stitch close to the outer edges of the door and windows. Draw the stems and window broken lines with a pencil. Using three strands of navy embroidery thread, embroider stems and window lines with stem stitch and leaves and door details with lazy-daisy stitches. Sew a button to the centre of the door with navy embroidery thread.

2 Pin and stitch the side panels between the front and back, finishing 1.5cm above the lower edges. Press the seams open. Pin and stitch the front, back and side panels to the base, pivoting the seams at the corners. Clip the corners.

Needlework box template

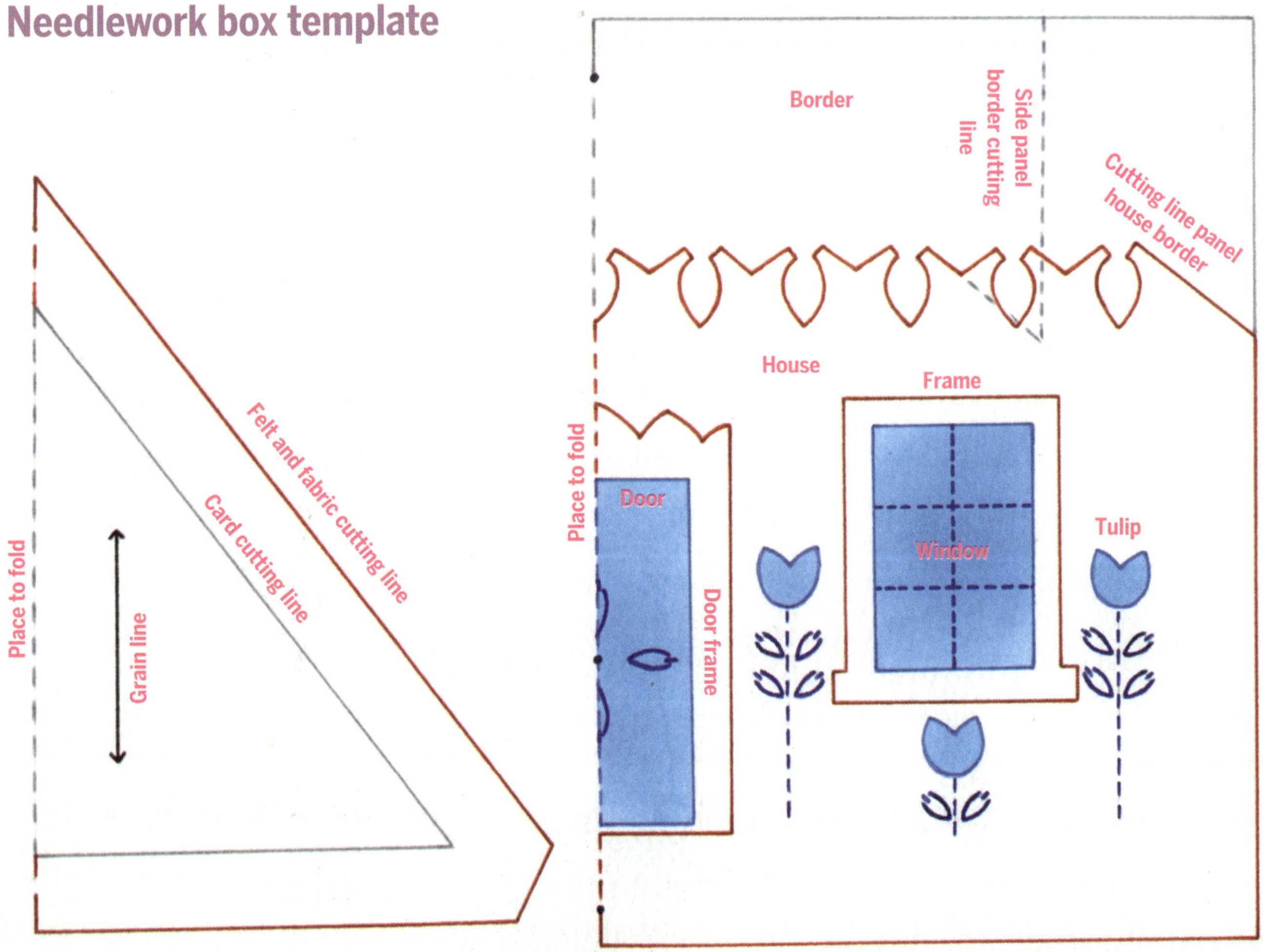

3 Turn the house right side out. Place the card base on the base, adjust the seam allowances on top of the card. Insert the card front, back and side panels into the house, slipping them under the seam allowances. Glue the upper edges of the house over the top of the card.

4 Tack the wadding to the wrong side of the patterned fabric pieces, then stitch it in place along the upper edge of the front, back and side panels.

5 Make the house lining following step 2. Trim the wadding in the seam allowances close to the stitching. Press under the upper edge along the stitching.

6 Insert the lining into the house. Pin and slip stitch the pressed edge to the upper edge of the house.

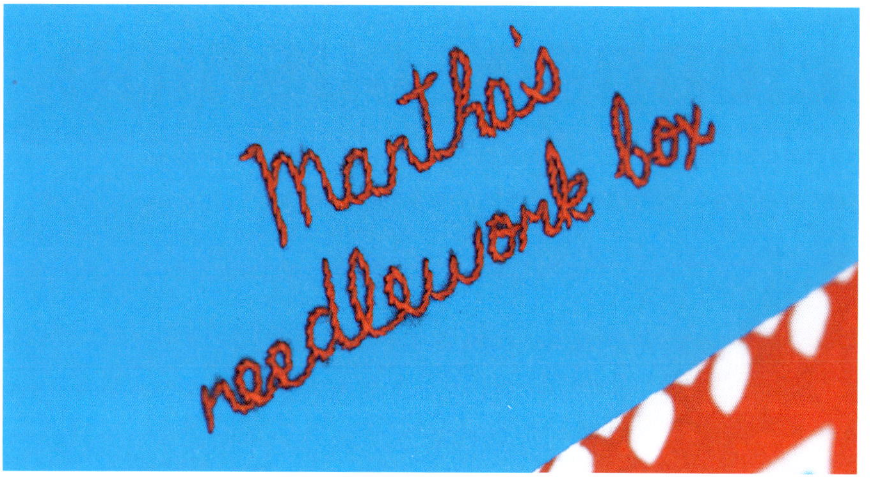

Making the roof

1 Use the alphabet (below) to write a name with an apostrophe 's' at the end on to tracing paper. Trace 'needlework box' centred underneath. Turn the paper over and retrace the writing. Pin the tracing right side up on the centre of one roof 4cm above the long lower edge. Dot a sharp pencil over the words to transfer them to the roof. Using three strands of red embroidery thread, embroider the words in stem stitch.

2 Pin the loops together. Top stitch close to long edges. Fold the loop in half and tack to the upper long edge of one felt roof.

3 Pin and stitch the felt roofs together along the long upper edges, starting and finishing 1.5cm from the short edges. Stitch the short edges of the gables to the short edges of the roof, pivoting the seams at the corners. Clip the corners.

4 Turn the roof right side out. Insert the card roofs and gables into the roof, slipping them under the seam allowances. Glue the lower edges of the felt over the card, folding under the fullness of the felt at the corners.

5 Pin and stitch the patterned roofs and gables together for the lining following step 3. Press under 2cm on the lower edge of the lining. Insert the lining into the roof. Pin and slip stitch the pressed edge to the lower edge of the roof.

Alphabet template

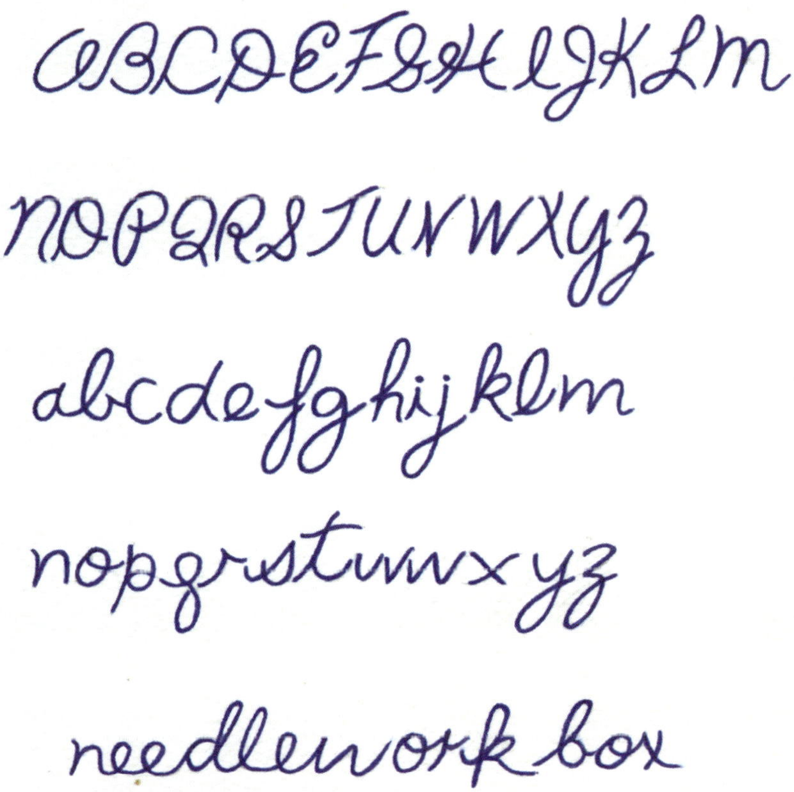

Enlarge on a photocopier to desired size

TOP TIP

For an elaborately decorated sewing box, just embroider the tulips on the sides and back of the house, too.

Elephant cushion

The perfect addition to any home furnishings, or a great gift for friends and family

You will need

Finished size: 40 x 40cm

- 50cm of 140cm-wide 28-count Cashel linen fabric in Blue Spruce
- 3 skeins of white stranded cotton embroidery thread
- Size 28 tapestry needle
- 180cm white pompom trim
- Matching sewing thread
- 40cm square cushion pad

Working cross stitch

Each cross stitch is taken over three threads of the fabric with three strands of embroidery thread in the needle. Each square on the chart represents 3 x 3 threads of the fabric.

1 Bring the needle to the right side at the lower left corner and insert it three threads up and three threads to the right, forming a diagonal stitch. Bring the needle to the right side three threads down.

2 To complete an individual stitch, insert the needle three threads up and three threads to the left, making a diagonal stitch. Alternatively, continue to make a row of half-stitches then work back, completing the upper half of the crosses.

Working the design

1 Cut a 30 x 30cm square of linen. Measure 6.5cm in from the left hand edge and 9.5cm down from the top edge. Start here by embroidering the tip of the elephant's tail (shown in red on the chart). Copy the chart. The square shown red on the trunk will be the end of the tail of the next elephant. Embroider three elephants in a continuous line.

2 Work the next row nine threads down, reversing the elephants this time so they face in the opposite direction. Repeat these two rows to make a total of four rows.

3 21 threads out from the elephants at each side and 36 rows from the top and bottom of the elephants, work a line of cross stitches.

4 When complete, press the work face down on a towel. With the embroidery centred, trim the fabric to a 27cm square.

Cross-stitch chart

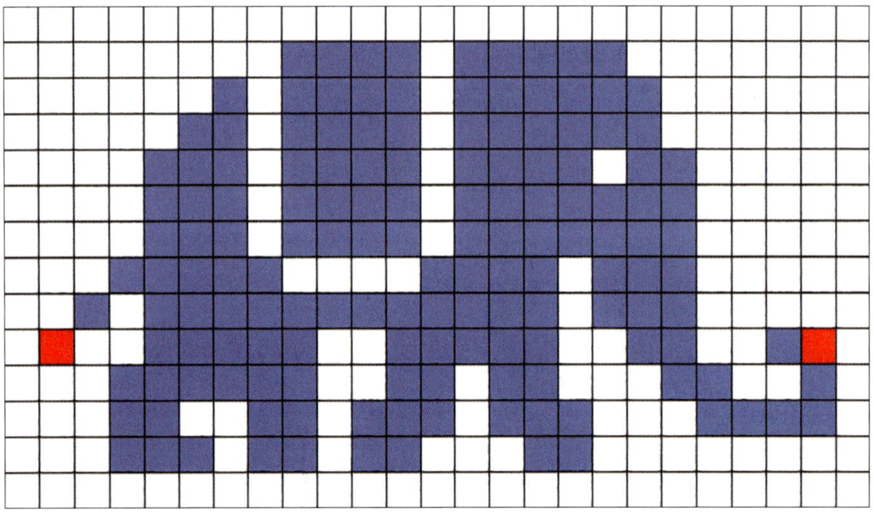

Making the cushion

1 Stitch seams with right sides facing and raw edges level, taking a 1cm seam allowance.

2 Refer to the diagram to cut two pairs of borders from linen. Pin the borders together in pairs. Stitch one diagonal edge, starting and finishing 1cm from the straight edges.

3 Open out the borders. Pin them together. Stitch the other diagonal edges, starting and finishing 1cm from the straight edges. Press all seams open.

4 Pin and stitch the short straight edges of the borders to the embroidered square, pivoting the seam at the corners. Press the seam toward the borders.

5 On the right side, pin and tack the pompom trim to the upper edge of the border, placing the top of the pompoms 1.5cm below the raw edge and 2cm in from the side edges. Cut off the excess trim. Repeat on each edge of the border.

6 Cut two 42 x 29cm rectangles for the back from linen. Press under 1cm then 1.5cm on one long edge of the backs. Stitch close to the inner pressed edges to hem the pieces.

7 With the outer edges level, pin the backs to the cushion front, overlapping the hemmed edges. Stitch the outer edge using a zipper foot. Clip the corners, turn right side out and insert the cushion pad.

Border template

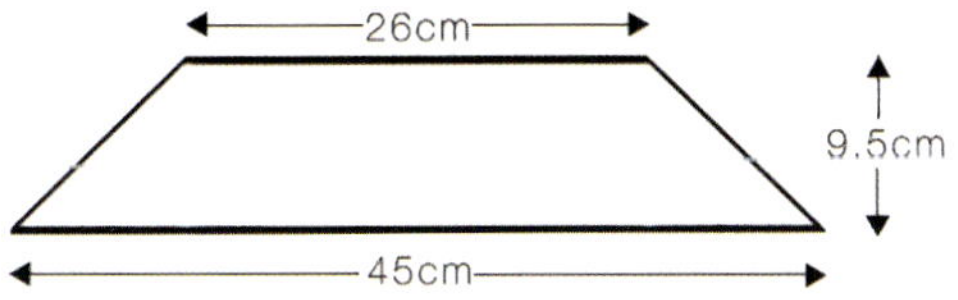

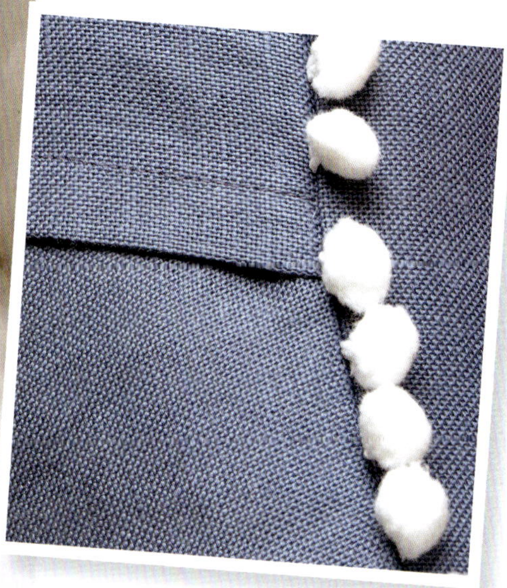

Make: Cheryl Owen. Photos: Barry Marsden

George the giraffe

Stitch up this colourful friend from the savannahs of Africa

You will need

Finished size: 26 x 16cm sitting

- Access to a photocopier
- Tracing paper and pencil
- Masking tape
- 25cm of 90cm-wide yellow felt
- 10 x 10cm square of brown felt
- Brown and yellow stranded cotton embroidery thread
- Two 8mm black safety eyes
- Four 1.5cm plastic toy joints
- Matching sewing threads
- Toy filling
- Large-eyed needle

Making paper patterns

On a photocopier, enlarge the patterns (right) to 240%. Trace the patterns onto tracing paper, placing the body on folded tracing paper, matching the broken lines to the fold. Mark the patches, notches, pleat lines, crosses, dots and dotted line. Cut out the patterns and open out flat.

Cutting out

Cut out two bodies. Cut one pair of heads, ears and soles and two pairs of arms and legs, one 6 x 2cm rectangle for a tail and two 3 x 1.5cm rectangles for ossicones (the bits that look like horns) from yellow felt. Cut one pair of ears from brown felt. Snip the notches. Mark the crosses on the wrong side of the bodies, and one pair of arms and legs with a pencil. Mark the position of the dots and pleats with a pin. Make a tiny hole at the arm joint crosses on the bodies and the eye, and joint crosses on the head, arms and legs.

Giraffe template

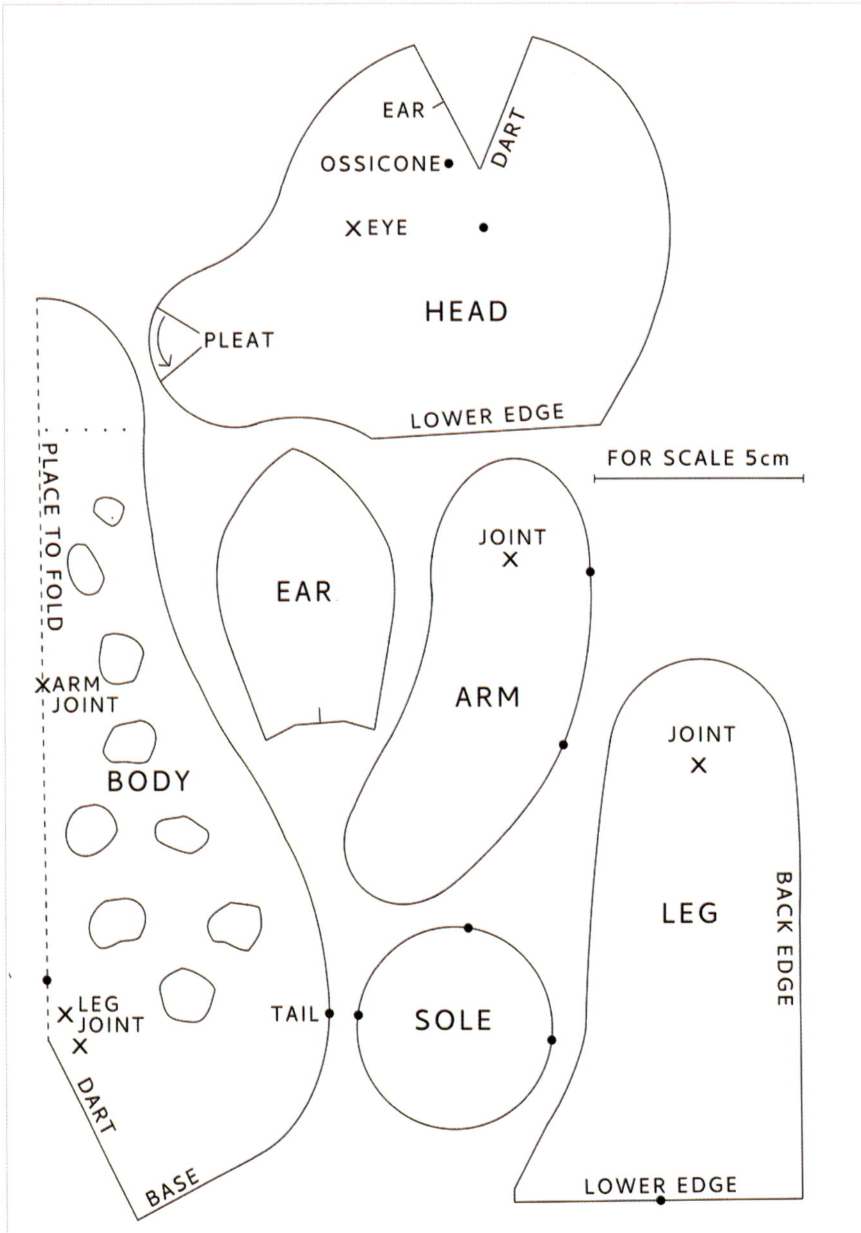

Enlarge by 240% on a photocopier

Feature: Cheryl Owen. Photos: Barry Marsden

Making the giraffe

Note: Join pieces with edges level, matching dots. Blanket stitch the edges with wrong sides facing, using two strands of yellow embroidery thread, making the stitches 3mm deep.

1 With right sides facing and taking 6mm seam allowance, stitch the darts on the bodies, leaving a gap between the leg joint crosses. Snip almost to the dart dot then press the darts open. Fold the tail lengthwise in half with wrong sides facing. Blanket stitch the long edges. With the tail extending outwards, tack 6mm at one end of the tail under one body at the tail dot.

2 Pin the bodies together and blanket stitch the edges, leaving a 6cm gap on the base and blanket stitching twice at the tail to secure.

3 Blanket stitch each brown ear to a yellow ear. With the brown felt inside, fold the lower edges to meet at the notch. With the brown felt facing the head, pin and tack each ear to the right side of heads.

4 Fold the ossicones lengthwise in half with wrong sides facing. Blanket stitch the long edges and one end. Tack the raw ends to the right side of the heads at the ossicone dots. With right sides facing and taking 6mm seam allowance, stitch the darts on the heads. Press the darts open.

5 Insert the shanks of the eyes through the eye holes and fix in place on the wrong side with their locking washers, pushing them down as far as they will go.

6 With right sides facing up, bring the pleat lines together then fold and tack the pleats in the direction of the arrow. Pin the heads together and blanket stitch the edges, leaving the lower edge open.

7 Insert the stalks of the joints through the holes on the arms and legs; the stalks will poke out of the right side.

8 With wrong sides facing, pin each arm with a joint to an arm without one, blanket stitch the edges, leaving a gap between the dots.

9 With wrong sides facing, pin each leg with a joint to a leg without a joint, blanket stitch the edges, leaving a 5cm gap on the back edge and the lower edge open. Pin the soles to the lower edges of the legs, matching the leg seams and dots to the dots on the soles. Blanket stitch the edges.

10 Stuff the arms and legs firmly with toy filling. Blanket stitch the gaps closed. With the arms and legs facing forward, insert the joint stalks through the holes on the body. Fix in place inside the body with the locking washers, pushing them down as far as they will go. Stuff the body firmly and evenly with filling. Blanket stitch the gap closed.

11 Stuff the head firmly with toy filling. Poke a finger into the head to create a cavity for top of the body.

12 Refer to the pattern to mark the dotted line on the body with a row of pins. With the head and body facing forward, insert the top of the body into the head. Pin the lower edge on one side of the head along the dotted line. Add more filling in the other side of the head, then pin that lower edge along the dotted line. Remove the first row of pins and add more filling, then repin the head. Blanket stitch the head securely to the body.

13 To make the tail fringe, snip light brown embroidery thread into five 9cm lengths of the skein. Thread one piece of the skein onto a large-eyed needle. Insert the needle centrally 5mm above the end of the tail, adjust the thread ends to hang level, then tie them together under the tail in a double knot. Repeat using two of the pieces either side of the first one. Separate the strands and trim to 2.5cm long.

Embroidering the bodies

Tape the body pattern on yellow felt. Draw around the pattern. Pounce a sharp pencil along the outline of the patches to mark them on the felt. Repeat to draw a second body. Join up the pounced dots to draw the patches. Using three strands of brown embroidery thread, embroider the outline of one patch with chain stitch, fill the patch with chain stitch, keeping close to the preceding line of stitches. Embroider each patch with chain stitch.

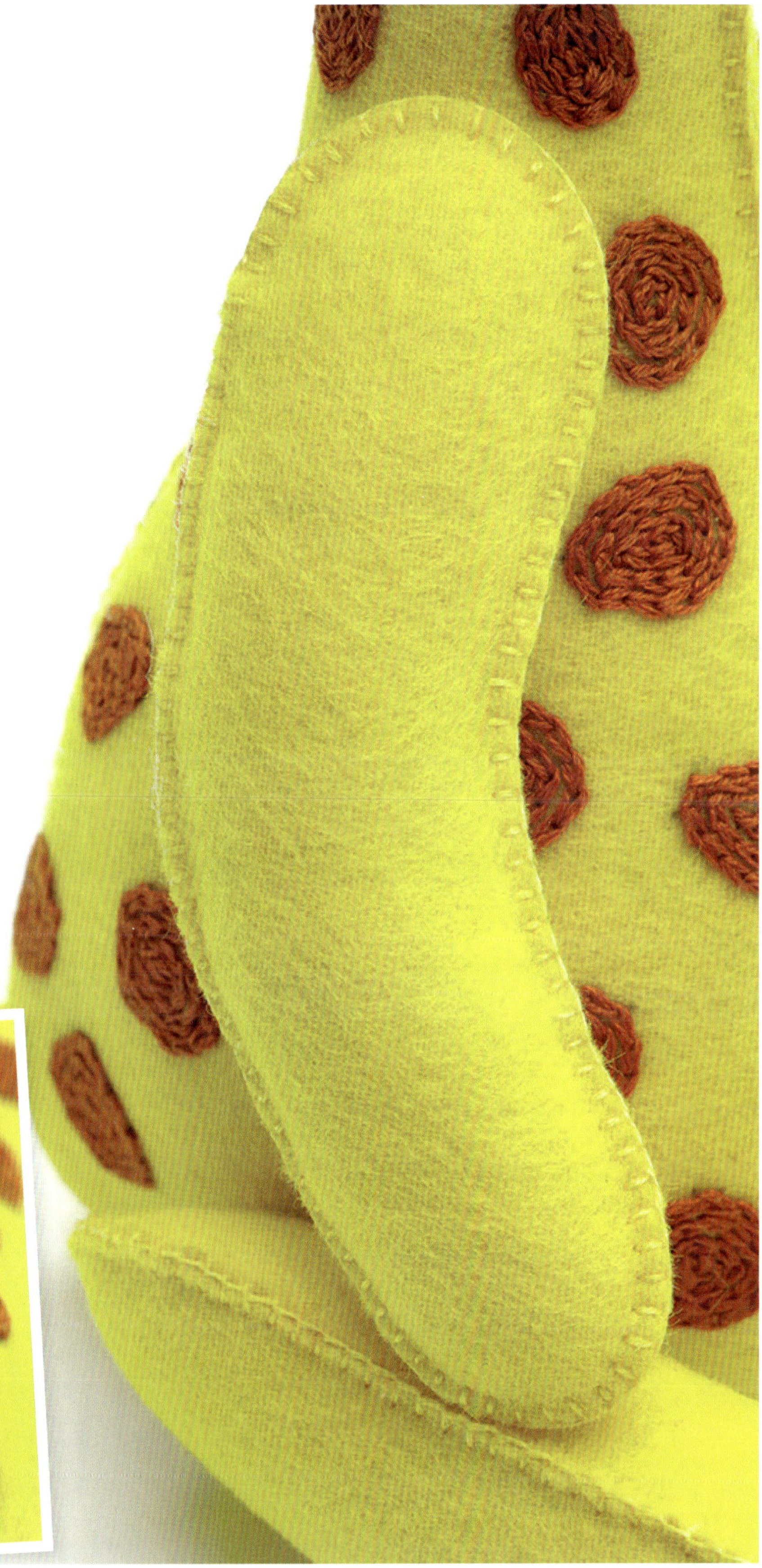